Scene by Scene
Film Actors and Directors
Discuss their Work

Mark Cousins

Published in 2002 by
Laurence King Publishing Ltd
71 Great Russell Street
London WC1B 3BP
Telephone: +44 20 7430 8850
Facsimile: +44 20 7430 8880
email: enquiries@laurenceking.co.uk
www.laurenceking.co.uk

Produced by McLean Film & Media Ltd

By arrangement with the BBC
The BBC logo and Scene by Scene
logo are trademarks of the British
Broadcasting Corporation and are
used under licence.
BBC logo © BBC 1996
Scene by Scene logo © BBC 1997

A catalogue record for this book is
available from the British Library.

ISBN 1 85669 160 8

Designed by NB:Studio, London
www.nbstudio.co.uk

Printed in Hong Kong

Dedication

Nobody could serve meatballs
like Jack Lemmon, one of the
real mensches of post-war cinema.
He died a few days after giving
permission for his interview to
be used in this book.

Contents

1

2

3

4

5

6

7

8

9

10

11

12

13

14

15

In the early 1990s, I saw a bootleg video called <u>Dietrich</u> <u>Songs</u>. In it, musical numbers from throughout the career of Joseph Von Sternberg's favourite actress were edited together in chronological order. There was no other action, context or commentary. It was roughly put together, with poor sound, but I've never forgotten it. Dietrich aged in the film, but also movie-making grew old, changed its photographic style, its lighting, its lenses, its ideas about women and song, sex and style.

There's song and sex, photography and lighting in this book, a similar historical montage. We start with Lauren Bacall wiggling to Hoagy Carmichael's piano playing and end with Tom Hanks on Omaha Beach. That's some kind of contrast, some kind of time line. In between there are forty self-contained film scenes, described by the people who made them. Many of these are just a few minutes from a conversation which then moved on. At no point during the interviews did we intend to extract them and string a history out of the results. That came later. Connections or repeated themes such as Brando, Pasolini and fear and chance in the filming process reflect what interested the interviewees most, or the caprice of their prompter, so please don't see what follows as any kind of planned history of cinema.

For a start it's western. There are no Japanese film-makers here, though it is one of the great film cultures. As these encounters were originally recorded for BBC television in the United Kingdom, they are filtered through televisual concerns; what people in the the United Kingdom one hundred years into movies have heard of and are prepared to watch. We pushed the envelope and talked of Bresson and Godard, Rilke and Joseph Brodsky, politics and James Joyce, but these were against the grain. Nothing better illustrates the randomness in the process than the selection of films taken from 1973, a year not previously considered a highpoint of movie achievement. Yet, <u>Don't</u> <u>Look</u> <u>Now</u>, <u>Save</u> <u>the</u> <u>Tiger</u>, <u>Pat</u> <u>Garrett</u> <u>and</u> <u>Billy</u> <u>the</u> <u>Kid</u> and <u>Mean</u> <u>Streets</u> reveal a cinematic year of great moral seriousness and the contrast to the representation of the 1940s with a few scenes from an existential comedy starring a certain Betty Perske (Lauren Bacall) is irresistible.

Figs.1-15 left to right, Scene by Scenes with Kirk Douglas, Jonathan Demme, Bernardo Bertolucci, Paul Schrader, Donald Sutherland, David Lynch, Janet Leigh, Sean Connery, Martin Scorsese, Rod Steiger, Roman Polanski, Jack Lemmon, James Coburn, Lauren Bacall, Terence Stamp.

The forty or so scenes were selected, with no strict criteria, from hundreds discussed in the original interviews. I've always felt that cinema should have its equivalent to E.H. Gombrich's book, <u>The</u> <u>Story</u> <u>of</u> <u>Art</u>: an elegant single elucidation of the history of cinematic style, the family tree of how Ford begat Kurosawa begat <u>The</u> <u>Magnificent</u> <u>Seven</u>; how Bresson led to <u>American</u> <u>Gigolo</u> and <u>Light</u> <u>Sleeper</u>; the baton passing from Sirk to Fassbinder; the bridge from Pasolini to Scorsese. The risks of dogmatism and forced comparison in such a book are great, of course, but the aim, to show how movie language has flowed between continents, is worth it. Many of the scenes in this book are here because they touch on such a history packaged for human interest with a tried and trusted punchline will deliver a few minutes entertainment, but shine no new light. Successful or otherwise and within the strict confines of television discourse, I have tried to push my guests beyond anecdotage. Many of them graciously acceded. Janet Leigh, Bernardo Bertolucci, Paul Schrader, Terence Stamp, David Lynch, Brian De Palma, Donald Sutherland and Roman Polanski are some that come to mind. Others stuck to the script.

Sean Connery was the first television Scene by Scene and surreally, we filmed it at my apartment. Jeff Bridges was the most recent of the twenty-three that followed. There have been too few women (I could drone on all day about how difficult it is to get women guests) and perhaps too many Americans (though, like Daney, I love American cinema). My wishlist includes many cinematographers, editors, writers and producers, as well as directors and actors. If the series continues, we might get to do some of them.

Hitting the twentieth long interview made it seem like time for this book. The acknowledgements at the back show how much this is not a one-man band, but I have to say that my prejudices show. It will be already clear that I think that movies aren't just entertainment. They also contain ideas. They are closer to architecture than novels, better at structure than psychology. Most American cinema is still a slave to the latter but, each of the US directors collected here – David Lynch, Martin Scorsese, Brian De Palma, Jonathan Demme, Paul Schrader and Dennis Hopper – has been as interested in the architecture of his films as their dialogue.

To say that cinema contains ideas is not to insist that it is serious. There are five musical numbers in what follows (perhaps Dietrich Songs was in mind), five comedies and six sex scenes. That whole distracted, ideological decade of the 1940s is represented by Lauren Bacall talking about whistling, wiggling to Hoagy Carmichael and by a roasting Warner Bros. cartoon which satirises her. Our 1950s is strangely baroque and exaggerated, but then it could be argued that the best films of the Eisenhower era reflected these qualities. The 1950s chapter starts with Kirk Douglas' hysteria in The Bad and the Beautiful, which Rod Steiger later picks up in The Big Knife, both bitter films about Hollywood and its stars. Janet Leigh talks us through some of the twists and turns of Touch of Evil; Jane Russell and Jack Lemmon talk about Marilyn Monroe. We have Lemmon, Terence Stamp and Steve Martin on walking like a woman. Nearly everybody, from Jane Russell to Bernardo Bertolucci, talks about the role chance plays in filming, and many emphasise the fear of being on a movie set. Our snapshot of the 1960s starts with three old-fashioned blockbusters, The Magnificent Seven, Dr. No and Spartacus, but Psycho cuts in like a shock. We have Polanski on the technicalities of Rosemary's Baby and then Pasolini,

Godard seen by Bertolucci and the revolution of Easy Rider. The moral seriousness of the 1970s films is accompanied by tears or great sadness in seven of the eleven films. American Gigolo, Raging Bull, Heaven's Gate and Dressed to Kill make 1980 the most schizophrenic year represented and for the 1990s we have Lynch's Bob, Goodfellas, Hannibal Lecter, Stamp's camp and Private Ryan.

As what follows was not originally written for the page, we have illustrated it more than most film books. In particular, we reprint key moments and gestures from each guest in the hope that they will animate the parallel text. Each scene is also described and key dialogue transcribed. It works best if you know the scenes. If you do, play them in your head as you read.

People regularly tell me that I have the best job in the world. Cinephobes would not agree, of course, but I drafted this introduction lying in the bedroom where James Dean slept at the Chateau Marmont Hotel in Los Angeles. Talk about close to the contours of movies, a place I want to be.

Mark Cousins

The "You Know How
to Whistle?" scene in
To Have and Have Not (1944)
Lauren Bacall (Actress)

p.14

1

2   3

8TH MAY 2000, AT A NEW YORK ART GALLERY

MARK COUSINS: Lauren Bacall, we're sitting in this very hot city of New York. People think of you as a Hollywood actress but you didn't stay in Hollywood for long.

LAUREN BACALL: No I only stayed there fifteen years. No, I know they think of me as a Hollywood actress which is unfortunate. I've never lived in Hollywood.

MC: When you lived in California, you and your rat pack friends tried to be anti-establishment...

LB: Well the rat pack came later. When I married Bogey... I was very lucky to have met a man like that because he had his feet so firmly on the ground. And he wasn't into the whole Hollywood scene. He wasn't cynical, but he knew the score. And he prepared me for it.

MC: Here's a very serious moment from the movies...

[Clip from Bacall to Arms (1946) a Warner Bros. cartoon parody of the "You Know How to Whistle" scene from To Have and Have Not. An ultra-sultry Bacall and a world weary Bogey trade sexy dialogue. In a cinema, various characters including a goggle-eyed, lecherous wolf, watch them lasciviously.] (Figs.2-3)

LB: (watches and laughs) Oh isn't it funny.

[Cartoon Bacall asks cartoon Bogart for a light and is thrown a blow torch. As she moves toward Bogart flames erupt from her feet. The audience goes wild.]

So funny. Some great likenesses actually.

MC: You became so famous that not only did they make films with you, but they made cartoons about those films.

LB: I know. That was extraordinary. I was nineteen years old. How do you handle that? You can't, unless you have a solid background, and I came into California with just that. I was only brought up by one parent, my mother, who was an extraordinary woman, and whose values were very clear. And my Uncle Charlie, and all of my family on my mother's side were very solid people and they had a great sense of fun... with all the wit and tremendous intelligence. All self-taught and self-made. My grandmother had brought my mother over from Romania. They'd been through a lot in Europe and they struggled when they got here. They came to the promised land but they made a life for themselves... And to grow up in that atmosphere is the best thing that can happen to anyone, because I was always taught the value of books. How important it was to read and how character was the most necessary factor in anyone's life... You must tell the truth. You must read the newspaper. You must know what's going on in the world and you must

look after your fellow man. You have to understand what is important in life so you don't go off the deep end. If it hadn't been for Bogey – first my upbringing and then from Bogey who continued in the same vein, because he believed everything that my mother believed – I can't imagine what would have happened to me. You can't handle that kind of success. Instant success. Totally unprepared. In every way.

MC: And did it damage you in any way?

LB: Well that didn't damage me... what damaged me was that I had so much publicity, so much coverage and became this instant star... it became far more than Howard Hawks ever expected. He tried all of his life to create a star out of an unknown and he never succeeded until he met me. And chose me, rather.

And it wasn't entirely lucky for me to have that kind of success because I could never possibly reach those heights again. When I was introduced to Moss Hart (the playwright) at '21' in Manhattan, he said, "you know of course that you have nowhere to go but down."

MC: I've now got the real scene that we've just looked at in comic form. Famously you say that you were very nervous when you were doing this scene. But, let's look, because there are no signs of nervousness. You look relaxed.

[The scene opens in close-up, as Slim (Bacall) kisses recent acquaintance Harry 'Steve' Morgan (Bogart) for the first time.]

MORGAN: <u>What</u> <u>did</u> <u>you</u> <u>do</u> <u>that</u> <u>for?</u>
SLIM: <u>I</u> <u>was</u> <u>wondering</u> <u>whether</u> <u>I'd</u> <u>like</u> <u>it.</u>
MORGAN: <u>What's</u> <u>the</u> <u>decision?</u>
SLIM: <u>I</u> <u>don't</u> <u>know</u> <u>yet.</u> (Fig.1)

LB: Mmm... Very cute. (laughs)

MC: Do you think of yourself as a comedienne?

LB: Yes I do, I think it's all a joke. I think life is a big joke and the joke is on us of course. I find myself constantly making a joke about almost anything. Whatever happens... death is comical, so many things are comical.

MC: Absurd, but not comical...

LB: But... I mean... but there's comedy because they're so ridiculous. With all the horror and sadness of them. I mean when the man from Forest Lawn (cemetery) said to me, "Would you like to see your husband, he looks wonderful?" I mean, you cannot... you say... please...

[Slim moves towards the door voluptuously and turns around.]

SLIM: <u>Okay,</u> <u>you</u> <u>know</u> <u>you</u> <u>don't</u> <u>have</u> <u>to</u> <u>act</u> <u>with</u> <u>me</u> <u>Steve.</u> <u>You</u> <u>don't</u> <u>have</u> <u>to</u> <u>say</u> <u>anything</u> <u>and</u> <u>you</u> <u>don't</u> <u>have</u> <u>to</u> <u>do</u> <u>anything,</u> <u>not</u> <u>a</u> <u>thing.</u> <u>Oh,</u> <u>maybe</u> <u>just</u> <u>whistle.</u> <u>You</u> <u>know</u> <u>how</u> <u>to</u> <u>whistle,</u> <u>don't</u> <u>you</u> <u>Steve,</u> <u>you</u> <u>just</u> <u>put</u> <u>your</u> <u>lips</u> <u>together</u> <u>and</u> <u>blow.</u>

MC: There's no hand shaking is there?

LB: But this wasn't the first day of shooting. I was nervous all the time though. And this was the scene they used for my screen test to get the part. I had to test for it because Jack Warner would not give an unknown a part like that. So Howard directed it. We did it with an actor called John Ridgely (lead in Hawks' war film <u>Air</u> <u>Force</u>, 1943). Then Jack Warner would not let me have the part, unless he owned half my contract. So Howard had to sell him half my contract.

MC: But how did you disguise your nervousness? How did you manage to come across as this very sexually confident woman, when you were nineteen?

LB: Nineteen and knew nothing... I mean really...

MC: I think we know what you mean...

LB: Yes. I had a great imagination, that's all I can tell you. 'The look' kind of came out of that because I found that if I held my head down and looked up, all this (moves her neck) was very tight and I didn't shake so much (Fig.4). So I did this (lowers her head again) and I did the cigarette and it was easier. It worked better for me as far as the shaking was concerned. But other than that, I just did the best I could because when I had to light a cigarette, my hand was going like this (shaking). But... if you grow up, especially as a product of divorce and an only child, your imagination runs wild. So you have this fantasy life and it's all play-acting... Playing this woman of the world at the age of nineteen, flirting with the guy and all this stuff. It was great fun. I was scared to death because when Howard would say, "Quiet on the set", then the bell would ring and he'd say, "Action" and then dead silence. All those people are staring at me and the camera... It's frightening.

MC: But you didn't crack?

LB: No. Bogey helped to steady me a lot too because he fooled and made jokes. He made me laugh and helped me some.

MC: How good an actor was Bogey?

LB: He was a fine actor. He was a theatre-trained actor. He was in seven hit shows in a row. He loved being an actor. He had great respect for his profession, for real actors, not for stars. And he grew up in the theatre of the Lunts, Noël Coward, Robert Sherwood and Leslie Howard and all of the most extraordinary talent. He was capable of playing almost any kind of part. If you think of his career, although he was cast as a heavy in the beginning, he was wonderful at comedy. But the problem with movies is that the minute they see you in something you succeed in,

you become that character and they keep casting you in the same kind of part. And of course that's killing to a career.

MC: Howard Hawks says that he showed Marlene Dietrich (Fig.5) this film, To Have and Have Not, and she said, "Howard, you've copied me." And he also says that he showed you her film, The Blue Angel (1930), before you did this.

LB: I don't even remember that.

MC: And Jules Furthman, who wrote some of your best lines also wrote those very sexually ambiguous lines for her as well.

LB: Well that I didn't know... As far as I knew, Jules Furthman worked with Hawks mostly. And I asked Howard Hawks once why he used him as he didn't write the entire screenplay and he said, "If there are five ways to play a scene, he will write a sixth way." And of course that makes perfect sense and that's exactly what Furthman did. He always came around the back way and suddenly there was always a little surprise there. As far as Dietrich was concerned, never in life did I think I was copying her. I was not imitating anyone in particular. Certainly not her. I was not a fan of hers. So sorry.

MC: And famously Hawks asked you to lower your voice and be a kind of female Bogey. To make you more masculine.

LB: Yes, well his fantasy and boy he really had a fantasy, his fantasy was that he wanted me... he said, "Women have a habit when they get anxious, when they're upset, of raising their voices. I want your voice to remain low." I've always had a low voice. My mother had a low voice. My daughter has a low voice. It's not an accident. It's not a creation of Howard Hawks. But he wanted that to happen, he wanted the voice to always stay in the low register, no matter how excited or upset I was in any scene. He wanted me to be insolent, a woman who would do what Carole Lombard did. I would much sooner have been identified with her than Dietrich.

MC: Oh Dietrich was better than you suggest...

LB: No, no. I think Dietrich was a great movie personality but she had a gigantic ego and she did not appeal to me, that's all. But I enjoyed watching her in some of the movies. And... if you could see the light. She always had the right light on herself. I never knew anything about lights. I was stupid about that.

But Howard wanted a woman who could trade dialogue with a guy on equal levels. He didn't want to have anyone that was cowed by a man. And so insolence was really what he was looking for and of course that's very easy to play. You know you say, "Oh you're going to tell me..." and then it becomes part of your personality.

MC: I've got here the end of the film To Have and Have Not where you do this wiggle...

LB: (laughing) Oh you like the wiggle...

MC: I'm not saying this because you're sitting here, but it's one of the sexiest things in the movies.

LB: That's a funny thing, you know, isn't it...

[Mid-shot of Slim (Bacall) standing by Cricket's (Hoagy Carmichael) band and as she moves towards Harry, they start to play a Calypso. Slim starts to wiggle slightly in time to the music, never breaking eye contact with Harry. He takes her by the arm and both leave the scene, smiling. As they exit, drunken ship-hand, Eddie (Walter Brennan) follows, mimicking the moves.] (Figs.6-10)

MC: It looks absolutely fresh, not planned or choreographed...

LB: It wasn't.

MC: Did Howard Hawks tell you to do it?

LB: No I did it spontaneously when we were rehearsing. Howard liked it and wanted me to do it. Of course then you get a little self-conscious... But I studied dancing for thirteen years. I wanted to be a dancer, not that I consider that dancing, but any time I hear music wiggling comes to mind.

MC: In the 1950s you met Ernest Hemingway (Fig.11) who wrote the novel on which To Have and Have Not was based. Did you discuss the film with him? Did he give his opinion on it?

LB: No because he was a friend of Hawks, but I gather the movie does not have a lot to do with the book.

MC: Yes, your character in the book has her purse stolen, but in the film she's the thief... much more interesting.

LB: Well, that's Hawks, you see. And that's coming in the back door again with Furthman. But Howard was a wonderful movie director. And his movies will last, I think. He was never in the category of John Ford or John Huston, but he's pretty major.

MC: I think he was better than Huston. He also made The Big Sleep (1946) – a re-match between you and Bogey. Do you remember the scene in that film where you go to phone the police, Bogey takes the phone off you and says... "She's my mother..."? (Fig.12)

LB: Yes, but he loves that bi-play. Howard had sex fantasies beyond one's wildest dreams. You realise that all of these things were men and women sparring all the time, but always with humour.

THE BIG SLEEP
[Private Detective Philip Marlowe (Bogart) begins a liaison with his client's daughter, Vivian Sternwood (Bacall). This scene takes place in Marlowe's office as he stands by Vivian who sits on the desk, using the telephone.]

VIVIAN: Hello, police headquarters please. Hello, this is Mrs...

[He grabs the phone from her, then speaks into it himself.]

MARLOWE: Hello. What do you want please?
I called you... say, who is this? Sergeant Reilly.
Well, there isn't a Seargent Reilly here. Wait a minute, you better talk to my mother.

[Marlowe hands the phone to Vivian, she smiles.]

VIVIAN: Hello, who's this? The police! But this isn't a police station. Well if you know why don't you... Look, this is not a police station! What was that you said? My father should hear this.

[Hands phone back to Marlowe.]

MARLOWE: Hello, who is this? Yeah, but she just told you... Oh! You're the police. Oh! He's the police! Oh well, that's different. What can I do for you? I can do what?...Where? Oh, I wouldn't like that, neither would my daughter.

(Bacall laughs)

MC: But there were darker sides to Hawks' personality as well. You're Jewish and he was anti-Semitic.

LB: Oh definitely.

MC: Did that manifest itself to you?

LB: No, because I never discussed it. I was so frightened of him. He scared me so and I must say I was a coward. But he never directed it at me because I don't think it occurred to him that I was Jewish and I certainly did not announce it. He did make a few remarks that were not very pleasant, but I used to talk to my agent about it, who was the only Jew that Hawks allowed in his house. Slim, his wife, knew but not Howard, unless she told him. As he came nearer the end of his life, I don't think it bothered him. I think he changed a bit. But then he was... awful.

MC: Your first two major directors were Howard Hawks and John Huston. Howard Hawks didn't like Jews very much. John Huston didn't like women very much. You were both and yet you seemed comfortable in this very masculine world with these very masculine men.

LB: Yes, I know. It's interesting because I grew up without a father. I don't know whether it was my natural enjoyment of exchanges that had something to do with that.

Overleaf: Lauren Bacall in a 1940s publicity shot.

1950s

Banishing Lana Turner in
The Bad and The Beautiful (1952)
Kirk Douglas (Actor)

p.24

The train sequence, snuggling
up to Marilyn, the Del hotel
and "Nobody's perfect" in
Some Like it Hot (1959)
Jack Lemmon (Actor)

p.44

The "Just Two Little Girls
from Little Rock" and "Is There
Anyone Here for Love" numbers in
<u>Gentlemen</u> <u>Prefer</u> <u>Blondes</u> (1953)
Jane Russell (Actress)

p.26

The taxi scene in
<u>On</u> <u>the</u> <u>Waterfront</u> (1954)
Rod Steiger (Actor)

p.30

James Dean and the knife fight in
<u>Rebel</u> <u>Without</u> <u>a</u> <u>Cause</u> (1955)
Dennis Hopper (Actor)

p.34

The producer's outburst in
<u>The</u> <u>Big</u> <u>Knife</u> (1955)
Rod Steiger (Actor)

p.38

The opening shot of
<u>Touch</u> <u>of</u> <u>Evil</u> (1958)
Janet Leigh (Actress)

p.42

The "Just Two Little Girls
from Little Rock" and "Is There
Anyone Here for Love" numbers in
<u>Gentlemen</u> <u>Prefer</u> <u>Blondes</u> (1953)
Jane Russell (Actress)

p.27

16TH OCTOBER 1998, COUSINS'
APARTMENT, EDINBURGH

MARK COUSINS: In 1953 you go
to Fox to make <u>Gentlemen</u> <u>Prefer</u>
<u>Blondes</u> with director Howard Hawks.
You're such a big star by then that
you're allowed to bring your own
team with you... cinematographer
Harry Wild, your make-up man, etc.
What I didn't realise is that even at
another studio, Howard Hawks was
still working under your manager
Howard Hughes' instruction. Hughes
was still controlling your image. For
how long did he do so? From <u>The
Outlaw</u> in 1941 until when?

JANE RUSSELL: Well actually I
guess it was until <u>The</u> <u>Fuzzy</u> <u>Pink</u>
<u>Nightgown</u>.

MC: Until 1957. So for sixteen years...

JR: Because I was always under
contract to him. I never was under
contract to anyone else. I signed three
different contracts.

MC: In <u>Gentlemen</u> <u>Prefer</u> <u>Blondes</u>,
you're teamed up with an unknown
blonde called Marilyn Monroe.

JR: Well Hawks had asked for me
at Fox and Howard Hughes said,
"Well okay" Marilyn had never had
a dressing room before, so they gave
her her first dressing room and she
was a little peeved at the heads of the
studio at the time and she was very
nervous. My crew and I were family
and Shotgun, he was the make-up
man, was a crazy Texan (Fig.13).

He was a darling. And he would just
hand me my powder puff because
I always make myself up. And on
set I'd shout, "Shot!" and he'd say,
"Oh I'm coming madam, I'm coming
madam." And he'd come running
across and the others at Fox were all
looking like this, My God, she must
be a real bitch. They didn't know us
and they looked and thought... What
kind of people are these? What is she,
what's she like? Shot'd come in and
close the door and we'd both laugh
and scream and hug each other...
Marilyn was very nervous and she
was afraid to come out on the set.
She would get there much earlier
than I did. I would get completely
dressed in an hour and other actresses
would come in anywhere from 5.30am
onwards and you had to be on the set
at 9 o'clock. I would come in at 8am,
they would have my breakfast ready
and they would be rolling my hair
dry. I'd be on the set at 9am.

And Marilyn still wouldn't be there
and she'd been in since 5am or
5.30am. So her make-up man told my
make-up man that Marilyn was just
nervous about coming out. He said,
"She's all ready, but she's just..." and
Hawks was getting a little irritated. So
I would go by her dressing room and
I'd say, "Come on Blondie, let's go, it's
almost time." And she'd say, "Okay, all
right." And she'd get up and we'd trot
on the set and she was never late. But
later on I can understand what was
going on. The people on the set would
just sit there and get madder and
madder, instead of going by and
saying, "Come on baby, let's go."

MC: Do you think she was agoraphobic?

JR: Possibly. She didn't know anybody out there and she was working with someone like me, who had made a whole bunch of pictures and she was just nervous. And we became very good acquaintances. We were never that close because she moved to New York shortly after and that was not my lot, my studio lot.

MC: Hawks said that sometimes he would give you direction and you would translate it for her and then she would say, "Oh right, I can do that" as if you were her go-between. Is that true?

JR: Well, we were very friendly, and I felt like she was a little sister you could help along. The thing was, she had a coach on the set and instead of looking to the director after a take to see if it was okay, she would look to her coach. You don't do that with Howard Hawks, honey! So he put the coach off the lot. Marilyn would work all day and then go to her coach at night and work until maybe 10 or 11 o'clock at night.

MC: Hawks also said that he didn't direct the musical numbers such as "Two Little Girls from Little Rock" and "Is There Anyone Here for Love?" It was Jack Cole (Fig.14), the choreographer, who did the "Put The Blame on Mame" number in Gilda (1946) with Rita Hayworth and Some Like It Hot.

JR: Nobody directed Jack Cole but Jack Cole and he was wonderful. Marilyn and I started out learning the dance routines first. She would have been with her coach the night before and she would come in with no make-up on, to do the dance rehearsals. We'd work until I knew I was not learning any more, until I was getting a little cross-eyed, because neither of us were dancers. Jack had the patience of Job with us. He could bite the head right off one of his dancers, but with us he was patience personified. So when I was tired I'd say, "Jack I'm not learning" and he'd say, "Go baby, go, it's fine." And Marilyn would stay for another hour. She was very concerned about being good and then she would go with her coach.

MC: Men liked you in the films because of your beauty, but it's also interesting that women liked your films, particularly Gentlemen Prefer Blondes. Why? Is it something to do with that buddy protectiveness in the films? In "Two Little Girls from Little Rock", the opening song which I've got a clip of here, when Monroe's doing her bits, there's this sisterly look on your face, which is charming.

[Lorelei (Monroe) and her best friend, Dorothy (Russell) emerge from behind a blue curtain. They are dressed in scarlet. They perform in showgirl style. The song reflects the storyline of the film; two women trying to break away from the lives and loves of their past.] (Fig.1)

"Someone broke my heart in
Little Rock,
So I upped and left the pieces there,
Like a little lost lamb I roamed about,
I came to New York and found out,
That men are the same way
everywhere."

(Russell watches as she and Monroe perform the Jack Cole dances. (Fig.3) At a moment when Monroe sings solo, we freeze-frame and look at the expression on Russell's face.) (Fig.2)

"I was young and determined,
To be wined and dined and earnin',
And I worked at it, all around the
clock."

"Now one of these days in my fancy
clothes,
I'm gonna back home and punch the
nose,
Of the one who broke my heart [x3],
In Little Rock. Little Rock, Little
Rock."

JR: Oh, she was something else, she was adorable. But she would get her feelings hurt. Tommy Noonan (Gus Esmond), who was in this picture, played her boyfriend. He was a wonderful comedian. Anyway, after their first kiss, he went back and somebody asked him what it was like and he said, "I felt like I was being swallowed whole." Well she overheard that and burst into tears, went running into the dressing room… and it took forever to get her out. Now that's ridiculous. I would just have said, "You would be so lucky, honey." But… Marilyn was not raised around boys.

MC: That's why she needed you, the girl on the team?

JR: Well, there's a big difference if girls have been raised around boys or if they haven't. And the same with boys. Howard Hughes was never raised around girls...

MC: That explains the way he saw girls...

JR: Yeah. He saw them in a totally different way and it was just ridiculous.

MC: I've got here what is probably your most famous scene in the cinema, the "Anyone Here for Love" scene in the same film, with you and the Olympic team.

JR: My brother's in it! (Fig.15)

MC: I know, you touch his hair.

[Dorothy dances and flirts with an entire American Olympic team as they train. The men, dressed only in their trunks, ignore her and concentrate on their own exercises.]

"I like a beautiful hunk of man, But I'm no physical culture fan, Ain't there anyone here for love, sweet love." (Figs.4-6)

[As Dorothy sits by the pool, each member of the team jumps over her head and dives into the water. The last one doesn't jump high enough, clips her and pulls her into the water.] (Figs.7-11)

MC: That wasn't planned, was it?

JR: No it wasn't and they let the poor dancer who did it go. That was on a Friday and we had to wait all weekend and re-shoot the thing on Monday without my going into the pool, which is ridiculous because I was sure they were going to use the one where I fall into the pool and they did.

[Dorothy is gracefully lifted out of the water by the laughing Olympians and hoisted onto their shoulders.] (Fig.12)

MC: This scene is liked by gay audiences. It's very camp.

(Russell rolls her eyes.)

1

2

3

4

13TH SEPTEMBER 1999,
CALEDONIAN HOTEL, EDINBURGH

MARK COUSINS: In 1954, you made
On The Waterfront.

ROD STEIGER: Well, Elia Kazan, the
man who directed the film, I have no
respect for, at all, anymore. He sold
his friends in Washington to protect
his career and he was already a
millionaire in the theatre. There
was no excuse of a starving family
or anything like that.

Anyway he came to me and said,
"What the hell did you do on Sunday
in this thing called Marty?" (The
1953 Paddy Chayefsky TV play in
which Steiger played the lead). I
said, "I don't know, I don't know,
I'm amazed at the reaction." And he
said, "Will you go to Budd Schulberg,
he wrote a script called On The
Waterfront? You read the taxi scene
with him and if he likes you, you
can play Marlon Brando's brother."
Well, I almost fell on the floor
because Marlon Brando was doing
a magnificent performance in A
Streetcar Named Desire. My God,
this is... some colleague to work with.
And I went and read with Schulberg
which was difficult because he
stuttered. (And on that point, when
you work with somebody, after the
second day, if they are terrible or
they have a quirk, something you
are not used to, you must convince
yourself that it's part of their
character. If you don't, every
time they do this odd thing, your
concentration is going to go. It

takes you a couple of years to
learn that).

We went and did the scene and I
was very pleased, but a nervous
wreck. The rest is more or less
history. Sometimes I feel if I see the
taxi scene one more time, I'll shoot
myself because this scene has become
identified as one of the supposedly
great scenes in cinema. (Figs.1-2)

MC: Well, I hope you don't have a
gun because here it comes...

[Night. The back of a taxi which
has no glass in the windows, only
venetian blinds. Crooked lawyer
Charley Malloy (Steiger) asks his
younger brother Terry (Brando),
an ex-fighter, to do one more job for
gangster union boss Johnny Friendly
(Lee J. Cobb).]

CHARLEY: Listen to me, Terry. Take
the job. Just take it. No questions...

[Charley pushes a gun into his
younger brother's stomach. Terry
shakes his head in pity.]

...Terry, take the job, please. Please
take it.
TERRY: (shamefully) Charley, oh
Charley. Woh...

[Charley sits back, puts the gun away
and pulls himself together.]

CHARLEY: Look kid, I... How much
do you weigh? When you weighed 168
pounds you were beautiful. You could
have been another Billy Connor. That

skunk we got you for a manager,
he brought you along too fast.
TERRY: It wasn't him, Charley, it
was you. Remember that night in
the Garden, you came down to my
dressing room and you said, "Kid,
this ain't your night. We're going
for a price on Wilson." Do you
remember that?

[Charley doesn't look at him.]

This ain't your night! My night...
I could have taken Wilson apart.
So what happens? He gets the title
shot outdoors in the ballpark and
what do I get? A one way ticket to
Palookaville. You was my brother
Charley! You should of looked out
for me a little bit.

RS: The taxi was an old beaten up
prop from a television studio and
see the venetian blind? Originally it
wasn't there. When we walked on the
set the producer of the picture, Sam
Spiegel, and Elia Kazan were having
this ferocious argument. Kazan is
saying, "How the hell can I shoot the
scene if you can see through the back
of the cab and five feet away is the
wall of the studio? You were supposed
to get a back projection! And if I don't
have the projection, I can't shoot the
scene. I can't go in on a close-up with
Marlon like that, (Fig.3) you can see
that there is a wall behind!" The thing
that saved us was that one of the
working men said, "You know, I came
to work in a cab that had a venetian
blind" and Kazan, who is no fool said,
"Get me a venetian blind!" And they
put that in and we shot the scene.

The other thing is, it forced them to stay close, so the scene depended on the two actors. It also added a tension for us. Sometimes accidents or mistakes can add tension. If you can control your terror, it's very beneficial because, in my opinion, one of the greatest sources of energy is controlled terror, I can't do it, I can't do it, I can't do it but I will, I will, I will... and you do it. (Figs.6-8)

MC: And they are brothers. Charley is the lawyer...

RS: Charley is the weaker one. (Figs.4-5) He fell in love with luxury and the ladies and he loved the good life. He kind of sold himself. He didn't realise it at the time but it brought him into direct conflict with what was best for his brother. I remember I said, "How am I going to pull a gun on my brother?" And when you get to moments like that, it's best to let the scene take you where it's going... and I got so upset trying to save his life, that I pull the gun out and say, "You gotta go"...threatening him, hoping he says, "Okay."

Nobody knows what really went on in that scene. For example, we did Brando's close-up and I was off camera. When you are off camera, working with another actor, you do your nut, you overdo it, to help them with reaction. In a scene you might say, "I gotta tell you something, I hate you, I hate you." Off camera, to help the other actor, you say, "You are no good, you are stupid, you couldn't act if your life depended on it! How did you get in this film?" You know? Like that! Acting is reacting so we are very dependent on each other and when it was time for my close-up, that son of a gun Brando went home, and I never forgot that. It was like a wound. I couldn't believe a man that talented would walk out. Oh it's the lowest, I had to do my close-up with the stage manager, sitting with his script, mumbling.

So it must have burned his rear end when we came out even in that scene, you know?

MC: When you pull the gun, he just pushes it away with the tenderest of gestures. Is it that sort of tenderness between the two brothers which makes the scene so memorable, so moving?

RS: Well, first of all, as I understand it, one of the grips told Marlon a story about a guy who was challenged with a gun and in the story he just pushed it away. And being as talented and bright as he is, he took that right away. I didn't know he was going to do it. When I work, I don't like to know what people are going to do. It takes away from the spontaneity... What was the second part of your question?

MC: Why is the scene so memorable?

RS: Well... number one, because of Marlon's talent, but number two, it's almost a love scene between two brothers. I don't mean sexually, but there is such a feeling of simpatico between the two, even though one is doing something wrong. He's still my brother and he looks at me and I am still his brother. That added a certain compassion and intensity.

MC: When you were making the film, did it feel as if it was different from other movies...?

RS: No, that's a myth about acting. It's like when I did Marty, the actor is so busy hoping he can do it, he knows only a few things; it's a good script, good actors, good director, and that is all. You can't pre-judge anything in life, whether you are an actor or not. And so you just go one moment at a time, one scene at a time.

1

2

3

21ST SEPTEMBER 2000, WALKING
UP TO THE CHATEAU MARMONT
HOTEL, SUNSET BOULEVARD

ARCHIVE INTERVIEW
[James Dean sits in a office
discussing dangerous driving with the
actor Gig Young. He hauntingly draws
upon future events in his life.]

DEAN: I used to fly around quite a
lot and I took a lot of unnecessary
chances on the highways. And I
started racing and eh… now I drive
on the highways and I'm extra
cautious. People say racing is more
dangerous than on a highway.
Well I better be off.
YOUNG: Wait a minute Jimmy. Do you
have any special advice for the young
people who drive?
DEAN: Take it easy when you drive.
The next life you're saving might
be mine.

DENNIS HOPPER: I remember when
he did this. What's really interesting
to me is that everybody said how
suicidal James Dean was and what
he's saying there is what happened to
him. He had been given a ticket about
an hour before he was killed. He was
going 120 mph. He was in a car that
would do 170 mph. He'd been given
this ticket so he was going 70 mph on
a highway which was the speed limit
and a guy, Turnipseed was his name,
came in from the side. He came in
at an angle and there was a stop sign
there (Hopper acts out the scene with
his hands). It was dusk and Jimmy
was in a silver Porsche and the guy
didn't stop at the stop sign. Hit

Jimmy right head on. And Jimmy
died. But it was a total accident. It
was actually the other guy's fault,
because he didn't stop at the stop
sign. It wasn't Jimmy's fault at all.

MARK COUSINS: What was it about
him that impressed you so much? You
talked about him for years afterwards.

DH: Well I thought until I met him
that I was the best young actor in
the world.

MC: How modest of you!

DH: I was eighteen when we did
Rebel Without a Cause and nineteen
when we did Giant (1956). And I'd
never seen anybody improvise. I'd
never seen anybody mark out all the
indications in the script and suddenly
start howling in the police station
like a siren and doing the kind of
things that he was doing. When the
police were searching him, he started
laughing like they were tickling
him and these things weren't on
the written page. I couldn't imagine
where they were coming from, how
he was coming up with these brilliant
things. So I threw Jimmy into a car
and I said, I got to know what you're
doing, you know? I thought I was the
best young actor around. And so he
told me, he said, "You've got to learn
to do moment-to-moment reality."
And I said, "What is that?" And he
said, "Well, somebody says, 'hello' to
you, you say, 'hello' to them. And if
somebody says, 'Go screw yourself',
you go, 'Hey wait a second', you
know? If somebody opens a door and

they have a gun in their hand, you
should be able to react differently
every time. Maybe you start laughing
hysterically when you see the gun
pointed at you. There shouldn't be
any preconceived ideas of how you're
going to react. And these things will
become very difficult in the beginning
because you'll become aware that
you're doing them." And that meant
a lot to me.

I've never in my life seen anybody as
good an actor as he was. I mean that's
including Brando and Montgomery
Clift, which he told me. He said, "You
know, one of the reasons I know I'm
going to be famous is I have Brando
on one hand saying, 'Go fuck yourself'
and I have Montgomery Clift on the
other saying, 'Please forgive me.'
And somewhere in the middle is
James Dean." He filled himself up
with emotion and he was an
expressionist, he was a dancer. He
expressed himself physically. The way
he marks off the land in Giant or lifts
himself up on the water tower, just his
physical presence… He told me once,
"You can play Hamlet standing on
your hands, eating a carrot as long as
people, when they see your eyes, they
know that you're telling the truth."

MC: And if he was wise about acting,
where did he get that wisdom from?

DH: Well first of all he started out at
UCLA (University of California, Los
Angeles) drama department. He was
an extra on one of Rock Hudson's
films. He did a couple of Pepsi-Cola
and Coca-Cola commercials and so on

before he went to New York and studied with Lee Strasberg at the Actors Studio. And so when he came back to Hollywood he was aware of a lot of things that most people weren't aware of. He came back as a star with Kazan, who was the greatest actor's director of the time, starring in East of Eden (1955). He forced his way, he was going to do things his way and nobody was going to interfere with him. To see somebody having the courage of their convictions at that young an age and saying, "Acting is everything, acting is my life, culture is my life, art is my life, nothing is going to get in the way of it." To me, the most important thing that was ever said about creation was Rainer Maria Rilke's Letters To A Young Poet. He said that you must go back to your everyday life and find there the poetry to call forth and you must ask yourself in the stillest moment of your night, if it were denied you to create, would you die? And if your answer is yes, then you have no choice but to be an artist. And if your answer is no, support the arts and have a wonderful life, but don't try to create. And this was something that I've never seen, such a final commitment as James Dean's. He would come in days and you'd say, "Hello Jimmy" and he wouldn't even acknowledge you were there. Other times he'd be very gregarious and very outgoing, but these were times when he could allow himself to.

MC: I've got here the knife fight scene from Rebel Without a Cause. You are in the background. (Hopper laughs a little as the scene starts.) (Fig.5)

[The CinemaScope scene opens on the roof of an observatory in broad daylight. Jim (Dean) backs away slightly as his argument with Buzz (Corey Allen) starts to reach breaking point.] (Figs.1-3)

BUZZ: What are you waiting on? I thought you wanted action. You chicken...
JIM: (in a rage) Don't call me that!

[Buzz continues to jibe Jim, as he lunges at him with a knife. Hopper (as Goon) is amongst a crowd of spectators including Natalie Wood (Judy), Sal Mineo (Plato) and Nick Adams (Moose), who look on and heckle the pair as they take stabs at each other.] (Fig.4)

DH: My memory about the filming of that scene is sitting up on the balcony, reading An Actor Prepares by Stanislavski!

I'll tell you something that happened during it. Corey Allen, who is having the fight with him, catches Jimmy, and actually clips him. (Fig.6) Nick (Ray, director) sees that Jimmy's been hit with the knife and he says, "Cut, cut, cut." And Jimmy gets furious and grabs Nick and says, "Don't ever, ever say cut to me. I'll say cut if something's wrong. Don't you ever cut the scene. He really cut me and this is part of the scene and I want that reality." He was furious and walked off the set and it took a while before we started shooting again. So that was the kind of commitment that Dean had to his acting.

MC: So the actor's more important than that director? Maybe that's why you got into trouble with directors. You thought you knew more than they did?

DH: Well, when you're dealing with the Method... at that time it was a different way of working than most directors were used to. When I say that I thought that James Dean directed Rebel Without a Cause, in point of fact it was an intelligent director by the name of Nick Ray who allowed Dean... to block scenes and to utilise Dean's talent and make this movie. But the actors are in front of the camera and if the director is saying, "Cut"... because the actor's having a real response and has been hurt or whatever, that's the actor's call. It shouldn't be the director's call. If something's technically wrong with the scene, then the director should say, "Cut." Otherwise, protecting the actor gets a little schoolmarmish.

4

5

6

13TH SEPTEMBER 1999,
CALEDONIAN HOTEL, EDINBURGH

MARK COUSINS: In 1955, you made a picture called The Big Knife, which was set in Hollywood. Tell me about your character.

ROD STEIGER: Well, in The Big Knife, everybody said I was doing Louis B. Mayer, who was the head of a studio and supposed to be very cruel, merciless and unfeeling. But I wasn't anywhere near Hollywood, so I didn't know anything about him, except by hearsay. My characterisation came like this, months before, I had walked past a New York health club, and this man came out. He must have been at the tanning department. He was very tanned with silver hair wearing a black single-breasted mohair suit. When I read the part in The Big Knife, I remembered him and said, "Yeah, black mohair suit, silver hair (Fig.9) and a tan." Hoff is his name and he is merciless; he is in love with power. He might have a latent sexual problem because in the script, he is jealous of the wife of Jack Palance, the movie star. She comes into the room and he says, "What is the woman doing here?" And listen to the way he says it, like he was talking about garbage. One time I opened a lid of a garbage can, and there were all these little maggots, and that's what I thought of when I said, "What is a woman doing here? Makes me sick!"

And for other parts of the role, I couldn't figure out what I was going to do. When you are having a bad acting day, there's a game you can play, and it's very good. I went to a big department store, started on the first floor and I said, "What does men's perfume mean to Stanley Hoff?" Second floor – "What does women's lingerie... what do stockings mean?" Third floor – "What do toys mean?" The fourth floor – "Men's clothing". As I was leaving I noticed a box divided into compartments. There were tie-tacks, and all of a sudden in one box there was one in the shape of a silver question mark. I said, "That's right, he's a question mark man. He didn't even know himself, he's got all this going on, a homosexual thing or not", and I bought it and wore it in the picture (Fig.2). When I was in a scene and felt a little nervous, I used to rub it and the whole thing just came together like that. It wouldn't work for another actor, perhaps, but it worked for me. I always wanted to reshoot that picture because, now, I am at the age he could have been, maybe a little older... he was about fifty-five... fifty-eight... sixty years old.

It was interesting because in the picture, I left my sunglasses on. And after that, everybody began to leave their sunglasses on! The eyes are the most expressive thing. Of course I'm not stupid, I'm not going to leave them on for the whole scene, but when at times it works, it's sinister. It's like the mask of Zorro! (Fig.1)

MC: The most memorable scene, I think, is the one where Palance the movie star, who you are trying to manipulate, runs towards you and you go like this (wraps his arms around his shoulders).

RS: I didn't know he was going to do that and I heard this running. I was scared, you know! I went like that (same gesture) (Fig.4). See, that's where your intuition works and then my intellect said that's good for the character. That's a one-millionth of a second. Poom! And you keep it, keep it.

[The scene opens as movie star Charles Castle (Palance) and studio boss Stanley Hoff (Steiger) are arguing about Castle's refusal to renew his contract. (Fig.3) Castle runs towards Hoff in a rage, ready to hit out. (Fig.5) Hoff turns around and crosses his arms to shield himself from Castle who pauses.] (Fig.6)

CASTLE: Oh, you're so lucky. But if this was a movie, you'd been on the floor ten times.

[Castle slaps Hoff's head and Hoff slightly trembles in fear.]

CASTLE: Just a small token.
HOFF: I'll break you... I'll break you like...

[Castle snaps his fingers in Hoff's face.] (Fig.7)

HOFF: No, no, no. I'll let the law do it for me, this time. And you'll lose everything, lose everything! This is a scandal, a disaster and a ruin... (Fig.8)

1

2

3

4

5

6

27TH AUGUST 1999, L'ERMITAGE
HOTEL, BEVERLY HILLS

[A time bomb is planted on a car.]
(Figs.1-2)

JANET LEIGH: (watching) This
is the new version. They re-scored
it, re-edited it and restored it, all
from a fifty-eight page memo that
Orson wrote after seeing the studio
version. When I saw this new version,
I just broke down and cried because
it's what the intent was.

[Two people get into the car.]
(Fig.3)

...In this new version there is no
score underneath or credits. I mean
for the studio to put credits over this
opening historic shot!

[They drive off, the camera cranes
high and left.]

...And then to have the score rather
than the source music from each bar!
It took all night to do.

[Crane down to front of the car.]

...The studio had expected this to
be a nice little murder mystery, an
ordinary kind of picture. Well you
don't have Orson Welles and have
an ordinary anything. He could only
make it extraordinary. They just
never understood it. We felt we were
doing something very innovative. We
felt we were touching on new ground.

[Honeymooners, Mike Vargas
(Charlton Heston) and Susan Vargas
(Leigh) cross the road into the shot.]

MARK COUSINS: There you are.

JL: (watching) Yeah... Chuck and I
would make our entrance and as the
camera's pulling back, you have all
these people pulling the stuff out so
it doesn't show when the camera hits
that spot. This is a three block shot.

[They walk closer to the camera.
Susan's (Leigh) arm is covered with
a coat.] (Fig.4)

MC: And you broke your arm before
you made this film.

JL: (watching) Yeah... which is very
funny. I put a sweater and a purse
over it and I went in to see Orson
and he said, "I thought you broke
your arm?" And I said "I did." And
I took it off and he said, "Oh that's
no problem, we can hide that." And
he thought of having her play it with
a broken arm, but then I said, "You
know this is on her honeymoon...
with a broken arm?" He said, "that's
too weird, even for me."

MC: The film's eccentric enough.

[The crane shot settles at a US/Mexico
border crossing point.] (Fig.5)

JL: We get to where this border
guard is and the camera mounted
on the crane was coming toward him.
It was his time and he would flub his
dialogue. And he would turn to Orson
and say, "I'm so sorry
Mr Welles."

BORDER GUARD: "You folks
American citizens?"

So Orson said, "When you're supposed
to say your line, just move your lips,
don't say anything... And for God's
sakes don't turn around and say, 'I'm
sorry Mr Welles'", and of course he
dubbed it in later. But that's the shot
we got and as we finished, pink started
to come up in the sky.

[The car's passenger says she can
hear ticking in her head. Susan and
Mike kiss. Cut to the car exploding.
Handheld track backwards as Mike
runs towards the explosion.] (Fig.6)

It was the first time I'd ever seen
a handheld camera used in a motion
picture. On news, but not on a
motion picture.

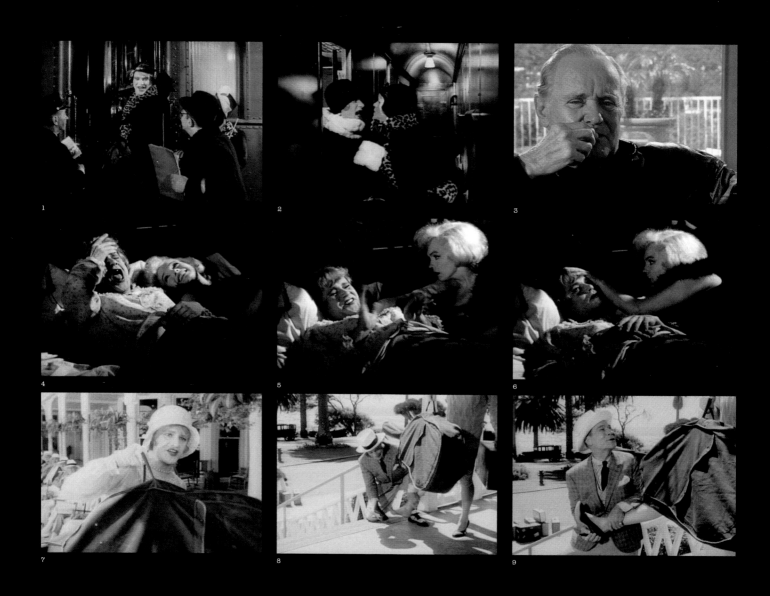

6TH MAY 1998, BEVERLY HILTON, LOS ANGELES

MARK COUSINS: <u>Some Like it Hot</u> was one of the first times that you pushed yourself creatively. At the time people must have thought that it was dangerous to do it.

JACK LEMMON: Yeah, if it wasn't for Billy Wilder, I don't think I would have done it, but because he wrote it and was going to direct, I felt it would be done with taste. He wouldn't get sleazy. I remember a couple of weeks into it I thought to myself, you're either in a classic or the worst comedy ever made. I didn't know which, except we were having great fun and I loved Billy. In the hands of somebody else, it could have been awful.

MC: At the time you were a studio guy, under contract to Columbia. Were you trying to get a broader range of parts?

JL: Well, it's lucky that Billy wanted me because, Oh Lord, at various times the Mirisches, who produced it, wanted Frank Sinatra, Danny Kaye…

MC: …Frank Sinatra in a frock?

JL: In his way, he might have been wonderful.

[The scene opens as Joe (Tony Curtis) and Jerry (Lemmon), dressed in 1920s fashion as Josephine and Daphne, board the train to Florida with Sweet Sue (Joan Shawlee) and her all-girl band. Jerry trips as he climbs aboard and Sue's assistant Beinstock (Dave Barry) pats him on the bottom.] (Fig.1)

BEINSTOCK: <u>Ups-a-daisy!</u>
JERRY: (annoyed) <u>Fresh!</u>
BEINSTOCK: <u>Looks like Poliakoff came through with a couple of real ladies!</u>
SUE: <u>You better tell the other girls to watch their language.</u>

[Cut to inside the train, as Joe and Jerry move down the carriage. Joe violently queries Jerry on his sudden name change from Geraldine to Daphne.] (Fig.2)

JERRY: <u>Well I never did like the name, Geraldine.</u>

[Joe lets go of Jerry's collar as Sweet Sue and Beinstock come up behind them.]

[Inside a carriage, girls are getting undressed, digging through their cases, chatting etc.]

JERRY: (merrily) <u>Hi, I'm the base fiddle. Just call me Daphne!</u>
GIRLS: <u>(in a chorus) Hi!</u>
JOE: <u>My name is Josephine. Sax.</u>
GIRLS: <u>Hi!</u>
GIRL 1: <u>Take off your corsets and spread out!</u>
JERRY: <u>Oh I don't wear one myself.</u>
GIRL 2: <u>Don't you bulge?</u>
JERRY: <u>Bulge? Me?</u>

[Jerry sits down beside the girl, making himself comfortable.]

<u>I just have the most divine seamstress, comes in once a month. My dear she's just so inexpensive and she told me…</u>
JOE: <u>Come on Daphne!</u>
JERRY: <u>Oh, alright.</u>

(Lemmon laughs.)

MC: That scene shows clearly the way your character became one of the girls, more than Curtis'.

JL: Yes, he really believes it after a while. Later on my character gets engaged to Joe E. Brown and when Tony says to me, "How can you do that?", I say, "What's the matter? Guys get engaged to girls all the time." Then he replies, "Yeah, but you're not a girl, you're a guy." I say, "I'm a guy, I'm a guy, I'm a guy." I have to convince myself because I've talked myself into it, like an actor talking himself into a part.

MC: You become one of the girls, yet look less like a woman than Curtis does. You're make-up is more comic isn't it? Those bee sting lips!

JL: Oh we worked like mad on the make-up. I had a crazy guy named Harry Ray. Emile La Vigne, who was a very good make-up artist, did Tony. We worked side by side every day for a week, trying wigs and different make-up styles. Finally I said to Harry, "I'm thinking about my mother, when I was very, very young." It was after the flapper days of the 20s and 30s. I said, "Try bee sting lips", (Fig.3) so he did bee sting lips and I sort of pursed them, looked at them and liked it. Then we arched the eyebrows and moved them up a little bit and then I put a wig on that reminded me of the way my mother looked when I was a kid.

She thought it was a hoot and came down to the set. She took a look at me and let out a scream in the middle of the take. Billy turned and said (mimicking his accent), "Mother, vat are you doing?" She kept laughing all through the takes and I had to finally tell her to go and sit in the corner and please be quiet.

MC: But, there's a real lesson there: how important make-up is for comedy. Sometimes your lips are incredibly thin and sometimes they are huge.

JL: Yes, make-up is very important and wardrobe, no question. They help an actor so immensely. I remember once Larry Olivier telling me, I've forgotten what play he was talking about, but it was one of the classics. He was doing it in the West End and he was having great trouble, he couldn't get the part and it got down to the day of the dress rehearsal. He went to the theatre and it looked like it might rain, so he took his umbrella with him. When they broke for lunch he took his hat, put it on, took his umbrella and as he went out the stage door, started to twirl the umbrella. As he was twirling, he all of a sudden said, "That's him! I don't know why or what or how, but it is him." Everything else fell into place once

he had that image in his mind of that guy with the umbrella.

MC: I've got the scene from <u>Some Like it Hot</u> with you and Marilyn Monroe in the sleeper compartment.

[Sugar Kane (Monroe) snuggles in with her new found friend, Daphne (Jerry), who earlier protected her from getting into bother with Sweet Sue. Unaware that Daphne is a man, she indulges in girl to girl chat.]

SUGAR: <u>I'm not crowding you am I?</u>
JERRY: <u>No, it's nice and cosy.</u>

[Jerry giggles nervously and snorts.]

SUGAR: <u>When I used to share a bed with my sister, we used to cuddle up with the covers over our head and pretend we're lost in a dark cave and try to find our way out.</u>

[Sugar laughs.]

JERRY: <u>(increasingly nervous) That's very interesting.</u>

[He nervously rubs his head.] (Fig.4)

SUGAR: <u>Anything wrong?</u>
JERRY: <u>No, no, no, not a thing.</u> (Fig.5)
SUGAR: <u>You poor thing. You're trembling all over.</u>
JERRY: <u>That's ridiculous!</u>
SUGAR: <u>Your head's hot!</u> (Fig.6)
JERRY: <u>That's ridiculous.</u>
SUGAR: <u>You've got cold feet.</u>
JERRY: <u>Isn't that ridiculous?</u>

[Sugar warms Daphne's feet and Jerry groans.]

JERRY: <u>(mumbling) I'm a girl, I'm a girl, I'm a girl...</u>
SUGAR: <u>What did you say?</u>
JERRY: <u>I'm a very sick girl.</u>
SUGAR: <u>Oh, I better go before I catch something.</u>
JERRY: <u>(jumping up) I'm not that sick!</u>
SUGAR: <u>I have a very low resistance.</u>
JERRY: <u>Well Sugar, if you feel that you're coming down with something my dear, the best thing in the world is a shot of whisky!</u>

MC: Monroe was famous for doing forty takes or more, did she do it here?

JL: One take, one take, the whole thing.

MC: Why?

JL: She just got it. Billy said, "Marilyn, do you want to do another one?" She said, "No." And he said, "That's it, next scene." It was the first shot in the morning. I think it's the only time in her life she did one take!

MC: And it's a long scene, must have been about six pages...

JL: He might have covered it in one other angle I don't know. And it was not that she was not capable or that the director would cut, she would cut at times because she didn't feel right. Whatever it was, an alarm clock would go off in her brain and just say no and she would stop. We had one scene in which she walks into a room and says, "Where's that bourbon? Oh there it is!"(in a drawer), so Billy finally got "Where's that bourbon? Oh there it is!" and put it on all the papers, all over the place, on the sides of chairs, in every drawer and everything else. But she could never get all seven words out. She'd say, "Where's that bour...? Excuse me."

Now we got up into take 50, let's say, because it went beyond that and Tony says, "I'm telling you it's going to go to 60", and I said, "I bet it will go further." And he said, "I bet you 20 bucks." I won the 20 bucks. I think it was 62 or 63 takes, just on that.

MC: So you must have dreaded scenes with her?

JL: In a way, except I liked her very much and we got along great. I knew she had problems and that she was not happy. I didn't know why. It was none of my business, I never pushed it and we never got close enough for me to find out what her troubles might have been.

The biggest problem was not really that. It was her lateness. She would not come onto set to shoot until she felt ready and it was not temperament at all, it was a psychological thing with her. Until she could face that camera, she wouldn't do it.

MC: And you didn't know she was pregnant and that she had had a miscarriage?

JL: No, no... we didn't know it.

MC: It makes the film more poignant, I think. You once said that when you were playing scenes with her, it was like there was a glass wall between you.

JL: Then you'd go to the rushes and you wouldn't look at yourself, you'd look at her because it seemed like nothing was happening, but it was happening between her and the lens, not between her and you.

MC: Do you think she would have been any good in the theatre?

JL: I personally don't think so. I don't know, we'll never know, but I don't think so. I think she had a magic on film.

MC: When you were making this picture, you were worried that you weren't getting enough close-ups, is that right?

JL: Oh yeah. I worried in the first two weeks. I was aware that Charles Lang, the famous photographer, would use a key light for the two of us and then before we started, he would put a scrim over half the light, which was on me. Tony and I were together through most of the film, especially in the first half, so I worried that the scrim would draw too much attention away from me, to Tony. I didn't mean it selfishly, I just thought professionally, would this draw too much attention away from me onto Tony, who was brighter on screen than I was? I don't know if I ever told Tony this or not. So I went to Billy and said, "Charlie puts a scrim up over me, am I going to be too dark?" He said, "Of course not. I would never do that, that's on purpose. I don't think you need to worry too much about how you're going to come out in this film." So I took his word for it and it was fine from then on. I never even thought about it.

MC: But why did he?

JL: Because apparently it contrasted. It looked right. It just made me look slightly darker than Tony is, that's all.

[The band arrive at the Del hotel, San Diego (Florida in the story). Joe and Sugar walk ahead arm in arm, leaving Jerry to carry all the luggage. At the entrance sits a line of millionaires, one of whom Osgood (Joe E. Brown) takes a fancy to Daphne/Jerry. As Jerry struggles up the steps, one of his high heel shoes falls off. The gentleman immediately kneels down to retrieve the shoe.]

OSGOOD: May I?
JERRY: Help yourself.
OSGOOD: I'm Osgood Fielding the third.
JERRY: I'm Cinderella the second.
OSGOOD: If there's one thing I admire, it's a girl with a shapely ankle. (Figs.7-9)
JERRY: (quickly) Me too, bye bye.

[Jerry tries to make a get away but Osgood follows close behind.]

OSGOOD: Let me carry one of the instruments.

JERRY: <u>Oh, thank you. Aren't you a sweetheart!</u>

[Jerry throws all the instruments into Osgood's arms. As Jerry strolls into the foyer, Osgood struggles and staggers behind.] (Fig.10)

MC: (watching) Was your walk awkward on purpose?

JL: Oh God, it's on purpose. I've forgotten his name but Billy hired the world's greatest female impersonator to work with Tony and me before we began. He was French and they had to bring him over on a boat because he wouldn't fly. He worked for two days and then went to Billy's office and said, "I quit!" Billy said, "Why?" and he said, "Curtis is wonderful. Lemmon is impossible!" He said, "He won't do anything that I tell him correctly and he's just impossible! He'll never be able to play a woman and that's that and I'm through!" He got on the boat and went home. Well, one thing he did show me is that if you want to walk like a woman, you should not walk with your feet one beside the other, but cross them so you're walking like that (Figs.11-13). But I doubt I do that often in the film, because I didn't want to do it correctly. I thought it was much more important that Tony was better than me.

I was more interested in being funny than being correct. He was more interested in being correct and didn't give a damn about being funny. So I told Billy and he said, "Just do what you're doing, it's fine."

MC: Okay, last clip from <u>Some Like it Hot</u>, the ending.

[Joe, Jerry and Sugar dash aboard Osgood's boat, making an escape from the gangsters at the hotel. Joe and Sugar kiss and embrace in the back seat as Osgood and Jerry (still dressed as Daphne) sit in the front.]

OSGOOD: <u>(steering the boat) I called Mama. She was so happy, she cried! She wants you to have her wedding gown. It's white lace.</u>
JERRY: <u>Osgood, I can't get married in your mother's wedding dress. She and I... we're not built the same way.</u>
OSGOOD: <u>(smiling) We can have it altered.</u>
JERRY: <u>Oh no you don't! Look Osgood, I'm gonna level with you, we can't get married at all.</u>
OSGOOD: <u>Why not?</u>
JERRY: <u>Well, in the first place... I'm not a natural blonde.</u>
OSGOOD: <u>Doesn't matter.</u>
JERRY: <u>I smoke, I smoke all the time.</u>
OSGOOD: <u>I don't care.</u>
JERRY: <u>I have a terrible past. For the past three years I've lived with a saxophone player!</u>
OSGOOD: <u>I forgive you.</u>
JERRY: <u>I can never have children!</u>
OSGOOD: <u>We can adopt some.</u>
JERRY: <u>(giving up) You don't understand. Osgood. (ripping off his wig) I'm a man!</u>
OSGOOD: <u>Well, nobody's perfect.</u>

[Jerry looks bewildered as Osgood continues to gaze at his bride.]

JL: It's amazing how many people thought I said that last line.

MC: Yes. Izzy Diamond who wrote this film with Wilder, says that they weren't happy with that final line.

JL: No, they wrote a lot of different endings and when we started shooting, they only had two thirds of the script. In the eight, nine or ten films that I have done with Billy, they did not complete the script before shooting because Billy felt that it kept him cooking. He had to keep working each night on the third act. They knew where it was going plot-wise, but they did not have the scenes down on paper yet, nor the dialogue set. When it came to the final line for this, it's one of the few times we shot the last scene last, because in film, we usually don't. They didn't know exactly what the line was going to be and the funny thing is that later when it became so famous, neither of them could remember who wrote it. Izzy always says, "No that's Billy's line", but Billy said "Izzy said the line." I didn't say it anyhow.

What Billy said was, "Okay, lets put it in. We'll shoot it, we've got a couple of minor retakes anyhow for the day after tomorrow and if we don't like the way it looks, we'll change it." So they shot it, they liked the way it looked and boom, that was it.

Overleaf: Jack Lemmon and Marilyn Monroe in <u>Some Like it Hot</u> (1959).

10

11

12

13

1960s

Style and the knife fighter in
<u>The</u> <u>Magnificent</u> <u>Seven</u> (1960)
James Coburn (Actor)

p.54

The dream sequence in
<u>Rosemary's</u> <u>Baby</u> (1968)
Roman Polanski (Director)

p.78

The trip and campfire scenes in
<u>Easy</u> <u>Rider</u> (1969)
Dennis Hopper (Director/Actor)

p.88

Crassus finally
identifies Spartacus in
Spartacus (1960)
Kirk Douglas (Producer/Actor)

p.60

The shower scene in
Psycho (1960)
Janet Leigh (Actress)

p.64

The beach and casino scenes in
Dr. No (1962)
Sean Connery (Actor)

p.68

The surreal train conversation in
The Manchurian Candidate (1962)
Janet Leigh (Actress)

p.72

The rape scene and the
"perfecto" style in
Marnie (1964)
Sean Connery (Actor)

p.76

The seduction of the mother in
Teorema (1968)
Terence Stamp (Actor)

p.82

The Nosferatu scene in
Partner (1968)
Bernardo Bertolucci (Director)

p.84

20TH AUGUST 1999, L'ERMITAGE
HOTEL, BEVERLY HILLS

MARK COUSINS: After the war, you
drove from California to New York
and studied acting with Stella Adler.
What did she teach you?

JAMES COBURN: Style mainly. She
said (impersonating a grand lady),
"I assume everybody can act, otherwise
you wouldn't be here. We're going to
deal with style now."

MC: What did she mean by style?

JC: Style.

MC: Based on movement?

JC: That's part of it, but Restoration
has a particular kind of style.
Shakespeare has a particular kind
of style and each character should
be approached in a particularly
stylised way. She'd say, "Go to a
museum, look at the paintings and
find a style for yourself."

MC: That's very different from
the Method, which was a kind
of unravelling, a soul-searching.

JC: Yeah, well she assumed that you
could do all that stuff because that's
all rehearsal. You find out what's
inside and you present it outwards.
But that was the most dull, boring
acting, there was. The only guy who
could really do it was Brando. He had
a lot of style.

MC: And Monty Clift and James Dean.

JC: And they were stylists. They
didn't just do it, they stylised it. And
of course Brando studied with Stella
and the new school and also with
Martha Graham.

MC: So having acquired style, you
worked in television, got married,
had a daughter and moved back
to California. You were in Ride
Lonesome (1959) and then The
Magnificent Seven. How did you
get involved in that picture?

JC: You'll never believe it. It was just
a miracle. I'd seen Kurosawa's The
Seven Samurai (1954) when I was in
New York. It was the first Japanese
film I'd ever seen. It had this great
character and I thought, my God,
where do we get characters like that
in American movies? I took everybody
I knew to see that film. I went seven
days in a row.

Then, oh, it must have been a year
or two later, I saw Bobby (Robert)
Vaughn one day in a grocer shop
across the road from a television
studio, where I was working and I
said, "What are you doing?" And he
said, "Oh we're doing The Magnificent
Seven" and I said, "You're doing
what?!" I had no idea this thing was
even being put together. He said that
John Sturges was doing it and that
Steve (McQueen) was in it.

And I said, "Who else is cast?" He
said, "Well Jeez I don't know... Eli
Wallach's going to do a part and Brad

Dexter and I think Horst Buchholz."
And I said, "Has it all been cast?"
He said, "I don't think so." So I
told my agent and then went to see
Sturges. I walked into the room and
all over the walls was this storyboard.
The whole film was shot right there.
And he said, "Hi Jim, now let's see,
there's one part in the movie that
hasn't been cast yet." And I said,
"Oh really, what part is that?" "Oh
it's Britt, the guy with the knife."
And I said, "Is that the role of the
greatest swordsman in the world?"
He said, "Yes, yes" and I said, "That's
the part I want, man." Two other
actors were up for it so I went home
at 2 o'clock and said to my wife,
"I think I'm in with a chance to play
that thing I always wanted to do."
And Sturges called up at 3 o'clock
and said, "You got the role, come
on over and pick up your knives."

MC: Here it is, your introductory scene.

[Colour. CinemaScope image.
At a deserted railway station, a duel
is about to begin. It is between knife
fighter Britt (Coburn) and gunman
Wallace (Bob Wilke). A freight train
stands by. Britt appears to be sleeping
in the sun.]

JC: There I am.

WALLACE: (to an onlooker) Call it.
ONLOOKER: I don't want nothing to
do with this.

[Britt pushes up the brim of his
stetson, revealing his face. He stands
up and faces Wallace. Low angle shot

27TH NOVEMBER 2000, BEVERLY HILTON, LOS ANGELES

MARK COUSINS: Many people think of Spartacus (Figs.1-3) as your signature film. Is it the best film you made? Not quite?

KIRK DOUGLAS: Well Spartacus was one of the biggest pictures of its time. My company was producing it and it is very, very important to me because I broke the blacklist with it by using Dalton Trumbo (Fig.6) to write it and by putting his name on the screen.

In that picture we had Laurence Olivier, Charlie Laughton, Peter Ustinov, Tony Curtis and Jean Simmons. She always wanted to play the part, but I didn't want her to. I loved her but I said, "Jean, I can't cast you, it's your English accent. I want the Romans to have English accents, so you need a different accent." But I couldn't find anyone, so finally she played the part and was so good. But I liked that picture, because it was a difficult undertaking and in the end, when I broke the blacklist, I think it was one of the most meaningful things I had done in my career.

MC: On seeing the rough cut of Spartacus, Dalton Trumbo wrote a fantastic analysis, differentiating between what he calls the Large Spartacus and the Small Spartacus.

KD: You know all about that?

MC: This is the article here...

KD: Let me see that. Yes, he wrote about sixty pages.

MC: And to summarise it, Trumbo thought of Spartacus as a great man of history who tried to change things, whereas Kubrick (Fig.7) had a more fateful view, that people can't really change things, that Spartacus was like a cog in a machine. Is that fair to say? On which side did you fall?

KD: To a certain extent, the audience has to decide that, but I think Spartacus was a great man without knowing it. He was a person against slavery, he was a biblical person in promoting democracy. The Romans never wrote much about him, they were ashamed of the power he developed.

MC: Kubrick was brilliant at composition, at photographic elements, but, there is a kind of coldness, isn't there, a lack of humanity in some of his pictures?

KD: Yes. Kubrick is a brilliant director, but he is cold. We found Kubrick trying to do the book Paths of Glory (by Humphrey Cobb). I said, "Listen we won't make a nickel, but we must make this picture and we made it and it was brilliant, but Stanley Kubrick's pictures... his last picture, Eyes Wide Shut, it was not sexy it was cold.

MC: I loved it... I've got here a scene towards the end of Spartacus. Laurence Olivier, playing the patrician Crassus (Fig.4), finally confronts you after having trailed you for so long.

[The scene opens as Spartacus (Douglas) is chained up as a political prisoner. Crassus walks by, recognising him.]

CRASSUS: Spartacus? You are he. Aren't you?

[Spartacus glares at Crassus, refusing to acknowledge him.] (Fig.5)

CRASSUS: Gladiator, I am Marcus Licinius Crassus. You must answer me when I speak to you.

[Spartacus refuses. Crassus loses his temper and hysterically slaps Spartacus. Spartacus looks on, then spits on him.]

KD: You know, I just realised I don't really see my movies. I didn't see Spartacus for about two years after it was made and today I am so close. It's interesting.

When we first presented Laurence Olivier with the script, he wanted to play Spartacus! But the part he did play was so well done. When in that scene he screams, not many actors would dare to go overboard as we discussed earlier. It's very different from underplaying, which can give you a certain strength, but often monotony I think. Olivier was, I thought, a great actor. During the shoot I loved to watch Charles Laughton and Peter Ustinov manoeuvring as they played! Brilliant.

MC: Ustinov used to make jokes at your expense didn't he?

KD: Of course! Listen, when you are the boss... I love Ustinov. One joke he used to say is that in a Kirk Douglas picture you shouldn't try to be too good! And he was the only one to get an Oscar!

MC: It seems to me that some of the scenes in the film are slightly overwritten. For example, this one with you and Jean Simmons, where he talks about his dreams.

[Spartacus lies in the arms of his wife Varinia (Jean Simmons). Close-up on Douglas.]

SPARTACUS: I love you more than my life, but sometimes, even when you're there sleeping beside me, I feel so alone. I imagine a God for slaves. I pray...
VARINIA: What do you pray for?
SPARTACUS: I pray for a son who'll be born free!

MC: Do we need to be told that he dreams of a son? Don't we know that anyway?

KD: Listen, you liked Kubrick's last film!

MC: Shows I have no taste!

KD: Well no, no! First of all, there's so much to say. That movie should have been set in the past, not in the present: A doctor picking up a prostitute... unbelievable in this day and age, but when it was written...

MC: We could talk all day about that picture. We should stick on your films.

5

6

7

1

2

3

4

5

6

7

8

9

10

11

12

13

14

15

27TH AUGUST 1999, L'ERMITAGE
HOTEL, BEVERLY HILLS

MARK COUSINS: Orson Welles'
Touch of Evil and Alfred Hitchcock's
Psycho have very similar hotel scenes.
In each, you're terrorised, in each
there's a nervous young man. Both
rooms were designed by Robert
Clatworthy. The camera operator
(John L. Russell) in the first was
the director of photography on the
second... (Fig.1)

JANET LEIGH: Isn't it amazing...

MC: So surely Mr Hitchcock had seen
Mr Welles' film?

JL: You know, Mr Hitchcock and I
never discussed Touch of Evil. But I
can't imagine that he would not have
seen Orson Welles' picture. Being
(someone who) appreciated film, he
had to admire Orson Welles. It must
have crossed his mind when he was
getting ready to make Psycho. It just
seems almost impossible not to have.

MC: Here's a scene from Psycho
where you've stolen a large sum of
money. You're driving, it's getting
dark and the camera's square on your
face. As you look at this, could you
describe what sort of woman Marion
Crane was and what Mr Hitchcock
told you about her?

[The scene begins. Marion Crane
(Leigh) has been driving for some
time, going through the events of
the day in her head. She's been
questioned by a suspicious policeman.

It's getting dark and has started to
rain...]

JL: Look. Very little jewellery. The
dress was bought off a rack. It was
something that Marion Crane could
have afforded as a secretary. That's
why there's not a lot of make-up
and the hair is very simple. It's not
stylised and she's imagining all the
things that are happening.

MC: This is a guilt scene, is it?

JL: Well she's imagining now what's
going on back in Phoenix. It's all
going through her mind; what she's
done; what their reaction is going to
be; and what's going to happen from
here on.

I was taught from the word go that
you try to play a specific person. You
have to give that character a persona.
And so to me, Marion Crane was a
normal kind of girl. She sang in the
church choir, she was a good student,
she was a good daughter. Her parents
were killed so she had to give up the
idea of going to college to support her
younger sister, so she went to work.
She forfeited young love, maybe she
would have been married and had
children by this time... This is my
scenario, nothing to do with the movie.

MC: Not in the script or in the book...

JL: No, not in either one. This is just
what I wanted Marion to be. She's
really a decent person, but her life,
she can see now, is slipping away.

[The driving scene continues. Marion,
being anxious about the late hour
and the bad weather, decides to find
a lodging.]

She's thirty, thirty-one and she meets
Sam Loomis (John Gavin) who is
caught in this trap of alimony and he
can't get out of it. So they have these
trysts and she's a passionate woman
and they mean a lot to her, but she's
also decent. She realises she can't go
on like this.

It's like her life is over, then all of a
sudden this obnoxious oil man comes
in and there's $40,000 given to her
to deposit. She's not a thief. She's a
terrible thief. It's like someone's given
her a pass to a chance of happiness
and she's torn – Should she?
Shouldn't she? Should she? Shouldn't
she? – and when she decides, you
notice it goes from the white bra to
the black bra, because she's decided
to do it.

But even then, she's not really sure.
She keeps looking at the bag that has
the money in it on the bed and she's
saying, can I do this, can I really?
Is it possible that I can go through
with this? And that's why she is a
terrible thief. I mean she couldn't be
more obvious! It's against everything
she believes in, but it's a chance
for happiness.

MC: What was she going to do with
that money? How did you imagine
that? Was she going to buy a house
with Sam?

15TH MARCH 1997, COUSINS' APARTMENT, EDINBURGH

MARK COUSINS: In 1962, you became a superstar.

SEAN CONNERY: This sounds like <u>This</u> <u>is</u> <u>Your</u> <u>Life</u>!

MC: You became James Bond (Fig.5) or as the Italians called him, "Mr Kiss Kiss, Bang Bang." How early did you realise what size of phenomenon Bond would become?

SC: Well, I had no idea, as I'd never been there before. It was the same for the ensuing twenty years. I had no awareness of that scale of reverence and pressure and what have you. It was around the same time as the Beatles, the difference being that they had four of them to kick it around and blame each other. I made as many mistakes as anybody in dealing with the situation, because I never had a press representative or anything. I found it all a bit of a nightmare to deal with, but eventually I evolved to deal with it in my own way.

MC: Let's look at a clip from the first Bond movie, <u>Dr.</u> <u>No</u>.

[James Bond (Connery) has successfully made his way to Crab Key, the private island of Dr No. On the idyllic beach a woman's voice is humming "Underneath the Mango Tree."]

SC: Oh, with Ursula! (smiles)

[Bond hears it and looks for the singer. Honey Ryder (Ursula Andress), in a beige bikini, comes out of the sea.] (Fig.1)

MC: It's a dream sequence, isn't it?

[As Honey sings to herself, she drops one of the shells she's been gathering.]

SC: (watching) She's still as beautiful, actually, Ursula. I still see her when I go to Rome.

[She inspects her shells. Bond, amused, watches her, in close-up.]

BOND: (singing) <u>Underneath</u> <u>the</u> <u>mango</u> <u>tree,</u> <u>my</u> <u>honey</u> <u>and</u> <u>me...</u>

[His song startles her.]

HONEY: <u>Who's</u> <u>that</u>?!

SC: I didn't retire on the royalties of the record!

MC: In your close-up, were you actually looking at her?

SC: Yes, in fact, I remember that <u>Dr.</u> <u>No</u> was a very, very poverty stricken production in terms of finance.

MC: $1 million.

SC: Less than that, because the dollar was devalued at the time, so it came under. And in that very sequence, I remember Harry Saltzman and Cubby Broccoli (producers) were even out with spades, when we were trying to take the sand up the beach. We didn't

have the kind of expensive equipment that you would fly in and out, so we were hand-moving the sand. That's how much money we had.

MC: What did the film-makers do to you and what did you do to yourself to turn into Bond? First of all let's talk about visual things.

SC: The most important element in the whole Bond series, apart from Fleming who had written the stuff, was Terence Young (Fig.3), the director of this picture. Terence really had identified very much with the grand seigneur, the elegant backgammon, Turnbull & Asser. He took me on a trip to get our clothes and it was an eye-opener. The clothes budget was astronomical in proportion to the film, but he was right, to insist that the shoes were made by Lobbs; no cufflinks (Fig.2), special fold-back buttons, and I used a small Windsor knot (Fig.4).

And equally we shared a similar sense of humour.

THUNDERBALL (1965)
[James Bond opens a bathroom door. A girl is bathing in the tub.]

GIRL: <u>Oh</u>!
BOND: <u>Hello</u>.
GIRL: <u>Aren't</u> <u>you</u> <u>in</u> <u>the</u> <u>wrong</u> <u>room,</u> <u>Mr Bond</u>?
BOND: <u>Not</u> <u>from</u> <u>where</u> <u>I'm</u> <u>standing.</u>
GIRL: <u>Since</u> <u>you</u> <u>are</u> <u>here,</u> <u>would</u> <u>you</u> <u>mind</u> <u>giving</u> <u>me</u> <u>something</u> <u>to</u> <u>put</u> <u>on</u>?

[Bond lifts a pair of mules and hands them to her.]

SC: Strangely enough, there's a lack of humour in Fleming's writing. He was quite dour about that, but very bright, very erudite, a real snob.

MC: And he introduced you to Noël Coward?

SC: Yes, well, Noël at that time was living on Jamaica too. It's the only time I've ever been, I never got back again. Noël was asked to play Dr No and he was very funny about it. I became very friendly with Noël too.

MC: And what did you learn from him? Eloquence? Mannerisms?

SC: No, Terence was more the influence on that, knowing what we were going for, without going over the top. He wanted to keep it real, the threat of it all, the sexuality, the jokes and the physicality. It was coming in the wake of kitchen sink drama and so we wanted to have something that was still backgammon, Chemin de Fer, good food, beautiful girls, marvellous cars and luxurious locations.

DR. NO
[Bond escorts a red-dressed woman through a casino.]

BOND: Tell me Miss Trench, do you play any other games besides Chemin de Fer?

MC: Why was Bond so popular?

SC: Well, he was popular with men and women, which is unusual. But anyone who says that he knew that it was going to be one of those immeasurable successes is lying.

MC: Looking back, it seems that Bond was successful because he was such a free character. The only authority figure in his life was M. He was totally at liberty to indulge his senses.

SC: Well that's true, but then he had the other side, his diligence, running and getting fit, yoghurt and not smoking so many cigarettes. And I feel my criticism, if there is one, about where it's gone, is that it's too politically correct, not quite dirty enough, not quite rough enough.

MC: Do you mean the Judi Dench bit in Goldeneye (1995) where she says, "Bond, you're a sexist, misogynist dinosaur?"

SC: (laughs) Well, a bit of that. Something's missing that gave a little bit of spice at no cost. They started to get a little antiseptic.

MC: And then Bond escalated and you changed your contract with Broccoli and Saltzman so that you could do non-Bond films, but they had to be with them. Why?

SC: Well, a few reasons, apart from their greed. There was the problem of trying to accommodate another movie. If you are doing a Bond film and you have another movie coming up, the Bond producers have first call. If the

Bond picture overran, the next job fell through. That's why I changed it.

2

3

4

5

27TH AUGUST 1999, L'ERMITAGE
HOTEL, BEVERLY HILLS

MARK COUSINS: In 1962, you
did The Manchurian Candidate. The
story revolves around Frank Sinatra
(Bennett Marco) and Laurence
Harvey (Raymond Shaw) returning
from Korea. They've been brainwashed
to try and manipulate the political
situation, so that an extreme right
wing candidate can become president
and ultimately destabilise America.
You have this extraordinary scene on
the train, where Sinatra is travelling
home in civvies and you see him for
the first time. Tell me about it.

JANET LEIGH: Well, I had lunch
with John Frankenheimer, the
director, before we started to shoot the
train scene, which came about twenty
minutes into the picture. At lunch he
said, "Janet you've got a real challenge.
Larry (Harvey) and Frank (Sinatra),
they've had twenty minutes to get the
audience with them. The audience
now knows them. They know (or
think they know) what's happening
to Larry, and they identify with
Frank." Then he said, "You're dropped
in there and you've got twenty seconds
to get the audience!" And I said,
"Oh that's nice!" But it was, I think,
the most challenging scene that I've
ever had to play... Because what
Frankenheimer was saying is true.
It doesn't matter which way the
audience goes with her, but they have
to go with her. They either have to
think she's a red herring, that she's
part of it, or they have to think that
she genuinely wants to help this man

(Sinatra), who's reaching out for help.
He needs something. Instinctively she
says to herself, "I want to help that
guy. There's something there I like."
You know how you just get that
feeling about somebody?

So I really loved playing that scene.
And I must say, of all the stories
you may ever want to hear about Mr
Sinatra, my working story (we had
also been great friends for a long,
long time) was that there couldn't
be a more giving partner in a scene,
whether he was on camera or off. He
couldn't have been more professional.
People would say he would do only
one take. Well, my experience is that
if it needed hundreds, he would have
done them.

MC: Here's the scene. People have
compared it to Bogart and Bacall...

[Major Bennett Marco, upset at being
forced by the army to take leave,
sits alone on a train, obviously deeply
troubled. Fellow passenger, Rosie
(Leigh) looks on silently as he
nervously tries to light a cigarette.
Failing to do so, he gets upset and
storms out of the carriage. Rosie
follows him into the corridor and
lights him a cigarette.]

ROSIE: Maryland is a beautiful state.
MARCO: This is Delaware.
ROSIE: I know. I was one of the
original Chinese workman who made
the track on this straight.
MARCO: Are you Arabic?
ROSIE: No.
MARCO: My name is Ben. (Fig.1)

MC: This is striking dialogue.
You were one of the Chinese men...

JL: And, "Are you Arabic?"!

ROSIE: What's your last name?
MARCO: Marco.
ROSIE: Major Marco! Are you Arabic?
MARCO: No.

The fascinating thing about playing
this scene is that the mouth is saying
non-sequitors, but the eyes are
connecting and saying something that
makes sense. It's like, I'm looking
at you and saying, "Are you Arabic?",
but meanwhile my eyes are saying,
"trust me, trust me, I'll help you..."

ROSIE: Let me put it another way,
are you married?
MARCO: No. You?
ROSIE: No. I live at 53, West 54th
Street, Apartment 3B. Can you
remember that?
MARCO: Yes.
ROSIE: Eldorado 59970. (Figs.2-3)

"...Don't jump, I can do it, I can help
you. I can be there for you. Look at
me. Trust me." And you can see him
react to it. There had to be great
connection in this scene and maybe
our friendship helped. I felt I was
reaching him. If I said it's 10 plus 2,
it's 3, 4, 5, 6, 10, 14, 24... I'm saying,
"I love you. Take care. Don't jump.
Trust me, trust me, trust me." And
then when she says something like
the number and means it, he hears it.

It was great playing that scene with
a brilliant actor.

2

3

15TH MARCH 1997, COUSINS'
APARTMENT, EDINBURGH

MARK COUSINS: Most people
accepted Hitchcock roles without
having read the script, but not you.
Is that the case?

SEAN CONNERY: Well, because
I was very curious as to what it
was. At the time it was offered to
me, Grace Kelly was supposed to be
playing the other part... and then it
went to Tippi Hedren, so I said, "I'd
certainly like to read it." Not unusual
I thought, because I would equally
say, "I don't think I'm right for it, or
this is more American than I could
ever be." But I liked it and eventually
I had a terrific time with him.

MC: Were you worried that it was
controversial, because your character
is sexually aggressive and there's a
rape scene?

SC: No, no, not at all. I don't think
that I was concerned about that
kind of issue. His kind of preparation
for movie-making was second to
none in terms of what he wanted
in the script. He visualised everything
and I enjoyed working with him
enormously.

MC: What was the film's storyline?

SC: Well, it's about a girl who's,
from what I remember, I'm not very
good on the past, Proust is okay,
I'm not! She'd had a terrible time,
her mother had been a hooker and
I played a very wealthy Boston type.

She arrives as a secretary, steals the
money and then I go after her.

MC: And you're sexually attracted to
her because she steals the money?

SC: Exactly... Well a combination of
quite a few things...

[Young business tycoon Mark Rutland
(Connery) honeymoons with his
kleptomaniac and troubled bride
Marnie (Hedren). The couple argue.
Rutland storms into Marnie's bedroom
cabin on board a luxury liner.]

<u>MARNIE: If you don't mind, I'd like
to go to bed. I've told you the light
from the sitting room bothers me.
RUTLAND: Well we can't have
anything bothering you, can we?
He slams the door.</u> (Figs.1-2)

...This is the night of the supposed
consummation, it was their
honeymoon...

[She screams. He pulls off her
nightdress, then covers her with
his robe. The camera tracks in, then
cuts high. The music swells. Marnie's
face goes blank, Rutland lowers her
on to the bed. The camera tracks away
to a porthole.] (Figs.3-6)

...It usually ends with smoke coming
out of a tunnel!

MC: Look at that, they've really
shaved your eyebrows there.

SC: Well they did everything in my
first introduction to the "perfecto"

of Hollywood. I think they wanted
somebody like Cary Grant. The same
thing happened with the hairline,
which had to be perfect, with this
(hair) piece. Then the guy had a
special way of doing your eyebrows.

MC: Plucking?

SC: Yes, he did everything. There
could never be a suggestion, not like
today where everyone has the stubble
look... Anyhow, that was the mode
for Hollywood then... He always said,
whenever your question got a little
too involved, although I never had
too many problems discussing
anything with him, "Oh it's just a
movie" (Connery imitates Hitchcock).
In <u>Marnie</u>, he had some major
problems because he was producing
and directing and the blue screen
stuff was not working. He had to do
it three times and he had quite a lot
of flack from stuff that was not going
well. Jay Presson Allen (the film's
writer) was a marvellously dynamic
woman. She told me, when she
was young, she was so electric with
herself that she used to put cotton
wool between her toes. And she came
and was sort of watching and would
put Tippi off quite a bit. But in spite
of it all, it came out in a funny way.
It had a retarded, late recognition
for being a certain kind of movie.

The dream sequence in
<u>Rosemary's Baby</u> (1968)   p.79
Roman Polanski (Director)

6TH MARCH 2000, LA SALLE DES
FETES, MUSEE D'ORSAY, PARIS

ROMAN POLANSKI: <u>Rosemary's
Baby</u> is not an entirely serious movie.
It can be interpreted in two ways. I
shot it in such a way that you could
consider Rosemary as a person with
problems who is imagining it all.

MARK COUSINS: And you made
it more ambiguous than the book?

RP: Indeed. That's what I did. That's
why I didn't show the baby.

MC: Here's the sequence where she's
impregnated.

[Young wife Rosemary Woodhouse
(Mia Farrow) lies on her bed, drifting
between sleep and reality. The scene
cuts to silent scenes on a yacht moored
in the Mediterranean.] (Fig.1)

RP: (watching) This part is definitely
a dream. The second part of her
nightmare is happening for real.

[On the boat, Rosemary's dress is
opened. In their apartment, her
husband, Guy (John Cassavetes)
removes it.] (Figs.2-3)

MC: (watching) It's silent, the
beginning of the dream. Why?

RP: (watching) Because I think
there's something in dreams which
is different from reality...

[The undressing continues.]

It's sort of as if you've heard your
own breathing. I'm proud of using
it for the first time, because I've seen
many others made this way now...

[Rosemary is almost naked on the yacht
now, surrounded by people socialising.]

...I just remember what dreams are. I
think we more or less dream the same
way. What is also typical in dreams is
this fluidity...

[Rosemary lies on a bed. The camera
tilts upwards to reveal Sistine chapel
ceiling frescoes above her head.]
(Figs.4-5)

...there is a person and then that
person is not who they were, but
someone else.

[The camera tracks along the frescoes.
Guy appears as himself, then as the
devil.] (Figs.6-7)

...Today with digital technology, you
could do it ten times better...

[The impregnation of Rosemary
begins.] (Figs.8-10)

...but then we were limited with
what we had. I wish I could do this
sequence again, with what we have
at our disposal nowadays...

MC: The camera is very close to
the actors at times in that dream
sequence. Is it true that you put the
camera quite close to Faye Dunaway
in <u>Chinatown</u> (1974) and that had
the effect of making her nervous in

some way, it added to this jitteriness
of her performance?

RP: No, I put the camera where it's
required for the given shot. I do not...
just arbitrarily put the camera closer
to an actor's face. I put the camera
where I stand, usually.

MC: What does that mean, where
you stand?

RP: I stand and watch the action and
then I'm just trying to film it the way
I saw it. It's simple.

MC: Lots of directors don't get it
right, even though it's simple.

RP: Well, I think that the other thing
that people don't get right is that
you just have certain predestinations,
maybe I have them for this. I'm just
standing there and watching what
happens and that's why I say it's
simple. I don't understand why more
people don't use this technique, it
seems to me the simplest. Of course,
it depends on the subject, but I'm...
mainly an invisible witness to the
events and my camera follows me.
If there's a camera movement, it's
simply because I moved from one
place to another... There's no other
reason and I hate convoluted moves
which make you nauseous and often
interfere with the story.

MC: Somebody like Martin Scorsese
does very complicated camera moves,
does that mean that you think that
he's being too elaborate in the way
he makes his films?

RP: No, I think Scorsese's camera movements are logical, they also follow the sense of the narrative; they are not gratuitous. Sometimes, maybe he gets a little bit carried away, but every one of us does, because you find some set extremely enticing and you just choose a route which is longer than it should be in proportion to the rest of the movie. But these are little sins, very forgivable! Indulgences, I would say.

MC: It also adds to the pleasure of the film, doesn't it? Something that's beautiful just for the sake of it?

RP: Yeah, but it's not beautiful if the proportion is ruined... you just have to have a certain composition.

MC: You read this book, Eye and Brain (by Richard L. Gregory), before making Rosemary's Baby and apparently were very influenced by it. How?

RP: Oh... I could explain it to you in many ways about perspective, etc. This book is a bible for me really.

MC: On perspective, for example, what did you learn?

RP: Well, perspective works differently in your eye than on the screen. In life, we have some device in our brain that compensates scaling. When you look at your two hands (holds his in line, one much further away than the other) and this hand is at the double distance, you should see it as half the size...

MC: You don't think it's a smaller hand?

RP: You don't think it's a smaller hand. If you photograph it, it will definitely look like a smaller hand and you'll have all those distortions that you have when you use short focal lenses. And I understood, doing Rosemary's Baby, how we can compensate for it, how we can use the wide-angle lens... and yet not having those silly distortions that you have in every music video today... So you can compensate for this... by slightly moving the camera. So you feel the depth, you understand?

MC: Yes.

RP: Most of the cameramen with whom I work think that changing the lens will change perspective. They think that there's more and more perspective when you have a wider angle. In fact, nothing changes, the angle of the lens only changes the size of the field of vision. It does not change anything in the perspective... Perspective only changes when you move the camera.

MC: So when our camera's static now, you won't get a sense of the distance between objects in this room... but when it moves, we get that sense. Is that what you're saying?

RP: Yes. Just moving the camera sideways a little bit (pointing to cameraman), what he's doing now, allows you to see behind me. When you use a zoom, nothing will change,

the background behind me will only go out of focus. It's so boring for you.

MC: It's not boring to me! In Rosemary's Baby, there's a scene where Ruth Gordon (Minnie Castevet) goes to makes a phone call. You seemed to frame her, so that we can't see all of her, she's half-way hidden behind a door. Why?

RP: It's much more interesting, much more mysterious, when you're sitting in a room and the person in the other room is going to talk to someone and you would like to partake in their conversation. If you see her in full view it's because the director wants the camera to be there and you have to make it a little bit awkward. Then you move the camera slightly...

10

11TH NOVEMBER 1997, FORTNUM & MASON'S, LONDON

TERENCE STAMP: Of all the films I've made, Teorema (Figs.4-9) is the one I'm asked to speak about most. Not a year goes by without somebody coming to me to say, "I'm writing a book about Pier Paolo Pasolini, can I interview you?" I met this great Canadian director Atom Egoyan and he said to me, Teorema is one of my absolute favourite movies of all time. And he just wanted to ask, "How did you do that?"

MARK COUSINS: How did you get involved with it?

TS: I'd been called back to Rome by Fellini to do the dubbing on Toby Dammit – Spirits of the Dead (1968), because his films have heavy post-synching. He makes his visual film and then he sticks onto it a radio play. So the sound is 50 percent of the film.

So I'd gone to Rome and my brother Chris who'd discovered The Who and was having this very successful career in rock and roll really wanted to meet Fellini. I took him with me, and we hung out together. One afternoon, I saw the amazing Silvana Mangano. I was looking at this woman whom I'd been in love with since Bitter Rice (1949) (Fig.1). She was with Piero Tosi (the costume designer) and saying to him, "Wouldn't Terence be good in Pasolini's film?" My brother was saying, "Pasolini, the great Pasolini!" (Figs.2-3) And I was saying, "What

about her? The great Silvana Mangano!"

[In a field beside a river, the mysterious visitor (Stamp) seduces young mother and wife (Mangano), for the first time. In close-up, she looks anxious.] (Fig.4)

And then after that meeting, my brother told me who Pasolini was and she spoke to him about me. So that's how I came to be in the movie.

[Bare-chested, the visitor has been out running in the field. He passes where the mother is sitting. She knew he'd come. She is undressed and has partially covered herself in a scarf. She looks up at him, he is crowned by sunshine.] (Fig.5)

MOTHER: Scusami, scusami.

[He kneels down, kisses her neck and they ease back onto the grass.]

TS: More. More! A great moment.

MC: Yes. And the story of Teorema is very unusual.

TS: Pasolini in fact really only spoke to me once. He said, "This is the story of the film: A boy comes to Milan. He stays with a family. In the family is the father, mother, son, daughter and the maid. And he makes love to all of them. This is your part." And I said, "Yeah, okay." (smiles)

[The visitor resting in the garden of the grand family house. The maid

(Laura Betti) looks at him and cries.] (Fig.7)

TS: He told Silvana, "He's a boy, but with a divine nature." And that was the clue I had. And I thought to myself, okay, he's a Catholic, he's gay, he's a Marxist, he's a poet, a very complicated guy. How would he view an enlightened creature? The thing that would appeal to him would be, "judge not." So that's what I did. I tried to keep myself completely in the moment.

MC: I think you've got to the nub of why this is a great film because you are at the centre of it, "judging not", yet Pasolini fiercely judged this family. He hated the bourgeoisie and thought that they were in inevitable decline. The combination is very strong.

TS: Yes. And my feeling was that he wasn't really a film-maker. You can't talk about how he shot something. He put the camera here, then he moved it there, then there. Then he just cut. But he was doing something better. He was using the camera to write poetry.

1

2

3

4

5

6

1ST DECEMBER 1998,
A LONDON STUDIO

MARK COUSINS: When you were eighteen, in 1959, you saw a film by Jean-Luc Godard who became a kind of cinematic father figure for you.

A BOUT DE SOUFFLE (1959)
[Parisian criminal Michel Poiccard (Jean-Paul Belmondo), waiting for American Patricia Franchini (Jean Seberg), sits in a large open-topped car. He buys a newspaper and reads it. A man appears in the background.] (Figs.1-2)

BERNARDO BERTOLUCCI: (pointing at the screen) Godard! Un coup de Hitchcock! (Figs.4-6)

[Close-up of a newspaper headline. Poiccard reads it. "No Trace Of The Highway Killer." The informer (Godard) turns and watches Poiccard.]

BB: Again!

[From behind their respective dark glasses and newspapers, the informer and Poiccard eye each other suspiciously. Patricia walks out of the New York Herald Tribune office towards Poiccard in the car. Jump cut and she's closer. Jump cut and she's almost in the car. Jump cut and the car door is closed.] MUSIC

MC: You said, that that film "changed everything". How did it do so?

BB: I remember in the 60s, I believed that I was ready to die and kill for a shot of Jean-Luc Godard. When you're young you can allow yourself this kind of rather extreme feeling. It changed everything... For example, the language.

[Close-up of the back of Patricia's head as she sits in the car. We hear a voiceover by Poiccard... (Subtitles)
I love a girl with a lovely neck... (jump-cut) Lovely breasts and a lovely voice... (jump cut) Lovely wrists, a lovely brow... (jump cut) and lovely knees... but who is a chicken...]

BB: A bout de souffle is the beginning of something. It was taking away all the weight that cinema had been accumulating and giving it a lightness of being, like a butterfly flying the streets of Paris and coming out with this conte morale, a short moral tale. And I became in some way, very close to Jean-Luc Godard between 1965 and 1968. It was more than seduction, it was plagiarism.

MC: And here is a scene from Partner, your most Godard-influenced film.

[Side-on close-up of Pierre Clementi's (Jacob) face as he sits in a cafe. He takes ear plugs out of his ears and we hear a voice speaking to him.]

BARTENDER: You can't sit here without drinking.
JACOB: I'm sorry I can't read with these plugs in.
BARTENDER: You mean you can't hear?
JACOB: Can't read.

[Cut to a close-up of his hands as he leafs through a magazine. He turns a page and we see a gun lying between the pages. He holds the gun between his fingers and casually moves it across the page. BLACK.
Cut to a wide shot of the same man seemingly hunchbacked, sitting at the same small table, leafing through the magazine. He pulls a vampire's face.]

MC: He's impersonating Nosferatu isn't he? (From Nosferatu, eine symphonie des Grauens, 1921, directed by F.W. Murnau.)

BB: Yes.

[On screen, Jacob continues his impersonation while outside a man quickly passes a telegraph pole. A girl appears and quickly pastes up a poster.] (Fig.3)

BB: That's a Vietnam poster. Just two kids passing by and putting up a Vietnam poster. (laughs)

For me, the 60s was where I was formed, I was shaped. Probably because having such a strong father figure, I was looking for a liberation from my original father figure and looking for other father figures... There was Godard, there was Pasolini (Fig.7). I'd been Pasolini's assistant on his first film Accattone (1961) (Fig.8) and that was maybe the most important experience in my life. Pasolini wasn't coming from cinema, he was a writer, poet, an essayist and he asked me to be his assistant, because he knew my father (poet

Attilio Bertolucci) and he knew my poems. I had an idea of cinema, I was a cinephile, I was a cinema freak, he wasn't. Because of that, I think that I suddenly saw Pier Paolo Pasolini inventing cinema. One day he said, "Facciamo una carrellata – Let's make a dolly track." I said, "A dolly!" and from out of the mysterious grip truck came this track and it was put on the dust of this Roman-like shanty town.

ACCATTONE
[The tracking shot Bertolucci describes.]

[We follow Franco Citti as he walks through the dusty Roman shanty town. Music, voiceover: (subtitles) "Poor Accattone, a man who's done for."]

BB: The camera moved on wheels. It was like seeing Griffith doing the first dolly movement and it was like inventing the birth of cinema, it was extraordinary. It wasn't learning from a great director how to make a movie, it was being there when a great intellectual, a great man invented cinema.

You know when I do a movie, I don't know what I'm doing, I am completely driven by my instincts.

MC: Maybe in the past, your films were too analytical? I know you feel this of the film we've just looked at, Partner.

BB: Yes.

MC: And several times, we've spoken recently and you've used the word "lightness". Maybe you wanted to make the cinema more like Ernst Lubitsch and less like Partner or Jean-Luc Godard?

BB: Lightness is just to take cinema back to its origins. You know what the Chinese call cinema? "The Electric Shadow", which is very beautiful. Cinema is shadow, cinema is air, cinema is light and shadow. The tendency is more and more to make it heavy and ponderous and very often, I'm afraid, pretentious. All I would like to do is to make movies, which really pass in front of the eyes like two butterflies flying, kissing each other.

But I don't accept what you said, "that Godard wasn't light", Godard was incredibly light. There's a scene from a Godard movie called Bande à part, 1964, where Anna Karina dances with Sami Frey and Claude Brasseur. That film is an example of how cinema can play with life and dreams. I was very pleased when I saw that Quentin Tarantino stole the entire scene from Bande à part and put it in Pulp Fiction (1994).

7

8

21ST SEPTEMBER 2000, THE CHATEAU MARMONT HOTEL, SUNSET BOULEVARD

DENNIS HOPPER: I was late taking LSD. Peter Fonda and all the other people had taken acid in the late 50s and the early 60s, but I'd had a very bad experience early in life with peyote... a cactus that the Indians eat for religious ceremonies. I took it and I saw the world like charred bodies and had this really terrible, terrible experience. So I didn't take LSD until I got the part of the pusher in The Trip which was written by Jack Nicholson, starring Peter Fonda, Bruce Dern and Susan Strasberg, my teacher, Lee Strasberg's daughter. And I took a trip. And I had a wonderful trip.

MARK COUSINS: And The Trip was made in 1967. It seemed like a whole series of endings happened. Martin Luther King killed, Bobby Kennedy killed. Nixon elected. And then you made a film about endings, Easy Rider.

DH: Yeah, right.

MC: And it was influenced by Bruce Conner films, is that right?

DH: ...Peter and I were at AIP (American International Pictures), and Jack Nicholson was also there. Peter made a film called The Wild Angels (1966), a motorcycle picture and Roger Corman made him a big star. Then Jack Nicholson made one, called Hell's Angels on Wheels (1967) and I made one called The Glory Stompers (1967). And we promised each other that we would not do a motorcycle movie, because we didn't want to become like singing cowboys and never get out of the motorcycle genre. Peter was up having dinner with the owners of AIP. At dinner Peter said, "I've got this idea for a movie" and he tells them his idea. "Dennis wants to direct it and act in it and I want to produce it and act in it. Would you give us the money?" And they said, "Yeah, we'll give you the money to do it."

So he calls me at 3 o'clock in the morning, wakes me up. And says, "I told Samuel Arkoff (chairman of AIP) and Nicholson that I had this idea for a film" and they said they'd give me some money. And I said, "What is it?" And he says, "A motorcycle... you and I. We take these dirt bikes and we go into Mexico, sell marijuana. We get these two gleaming bikes, ride across country (Figs.1-2) and we have a great time at Mardi Gras. And then we go off into Florida and we're shot by a couple of duck hunters.

I said, "I love the idea." So that's the way it started. Then Peter and I went on to his tennis court and we talked out the whole thing. We talked out from beginning to end. I put in the Jack Nicholson character because I wanted them to kill one of their own.

MC: And in the Mardi Gras section of the film, there's a trip sequence. Do you remember that?

DH: Oh, very well.

[The sequence takes place in a cemetery in daylight. People move around headstones, there is sexual activity, the lead characters displaying extreme emotions and there is a mysterious figure with an umbrella. The most striking image is of Wyatt (Fonda) embracing a statue, weeping for his mother.] (Fig.11)

DH: This is Peter actually talking to his mother, (Fig.10) because it's information I had about her killing herself. He's saying, "Mother, why have you left me, why did you leave me nothing but a piece of paper?" And I thought that the statue itself looked like the Statue of Liberty. And he started crying because I said, "I want you to talk to your mother, Peter, okay?"

The shots are diverse. Some are out-of-focus, others use extreme wide angle lenses, the images are stained at times and the light seems to be entering the camera.

This shot goes up the side of a crypt (Fig.12), it was an overcast day and everybody had left and walked out on me. I only had one cameraman and just a couple of people with me, because I'd got in a fight with one of the cameramen. We take the LSD and suddenly you see this flame-thrower go whoosh (acts a flash of light, which was in fact camera flare)... You actually see the wave of the sun, like this great flame, come down, which is a really powerful shot to me in this scene.

[On the soundtrack, women repeat biblical expressions.]

MC: Did you know when you were filming that this is what you wanted?

DH: Yeah. Well, it's primarily based on the Gospel According to Thomas… which is something that was found on the Dead Sea Scrolls in 1958 and it's just the sayings of Christ. In it there are things like, "They will call me the lord of peace, but I have come to cast wars and cause divisions until the world itself is set afire. For I am the fire, I am the light. I am the light that is above them all. I am the all."

These things are lines that I'd given them from the Gospel. That was the only real dialogue.

MC: And were you a Christian at this stage? Are you now?

DH: I'd been an agnostic. This was given to me by a prostitute that I knew in New York and it changed my mind about things. It brought me back into the fold. It became part of my work. The Last Movie (1971) also deals very much with the Gospel According to Thomas.

MC: How?

DH: Through the attitude. Both films deal with the concepts. He says things like, "If you don't hate your mother and your father in the same way that I hate mine you'll never be worthy to be a disciple to me. And if you don't love them in the same way I love them, you'll never be a worthy disciple to me." He says, "When I come back, I'll make Mary resemble you males", because the disciples asked Mary Magdalene to leave the room when they had business to talk. She doesn't have to leave the room.

MC: It seems to have really had an effect on you, if you can quote so much of it now.

DH: Well I read very little, so when I do…

MC: Why do you read very little?

DH: Because I wanted to… I believed in the senses… It says in the Gospel, "What you hear with your ears, what you see with your eyes, all the secret wonders of the world will be revealed to you. There will be nothing hidden to you…", and the only moral judgement it makes, is don't lie and don't do what you hate for all things are manifest before heaven.

MC: And do you feel you've done that?

DH: Yes, I think I have. To the best of my ability.

MC: I've got the scene from Easy Rider where Nicholson and you are talking around a campfire and it's one of the key dialogue scenes about freedom.

[Bikers Billy (Hopper) and Wyatt sit with their new associate, drunken Southern lawyer, George Hanson (Nicholson) around a campfire, in an isolated spot at night.]

GEORGE: You know, this used to be a hell of a good country. I can't understand what's gone wrong with it.
BILLY: Man, everyone's gone chicken, that's what happened to it. Hey, we can't even get into a second rate hotel, a second rate motel, you dig. They think we'll cut their throats. They're scared man!
GEORGE: They're not scared of you. They're scared of what you represent to them.
BILLY: Hey man! What we represent to them is someone who needs a haircut!
GEORGE: Oh no. What you represent to them is freedom.
BILLY: What the hell's wrong with freedom? That's what it's all about!
GEORGE: That's right, that's what it's all about alright. But talking about it and being it, that's two different things. I mean it's real hard to be free when you're bought and sold in the marketplace. (Figs.3-9)

MC: That seems like the crux of the film.

DH: Yeah…

MC: And who wrote it?

DH: Well, first of all, there's been this incredible thing about Terry Southern having written Easy Rider. Terry Southern didn't write one word of Easy Rider. Not one of his ideas is incorporated in Easy Rider. Terry Southern broke his hip, was unavailable, and the only reason his name is on the screen is because Bert

Schneider wanted it. Beyond that, Peter and I talked out the whole screenplay and they were supposed to write it while I was off finding locations with Paul Lewis. In the end, I got into a fight with Peter and Terry and kicked them all out of the office. I got a secretary and I dictated the whole screenplay to her in ten days and come out with, not a great masterpiece. Then, after that, 80 percent of the film is improvised.

This scene was written by me. That's the story. After that, unfortunately Terry didn't have a percentage of the movie. His name was on the picture and at that point he started calling me. But when it became famous, he started calling me and saying, "I want a percentage. I want some money. I'm having problems financially..." I said, "Don't call me, call Peter, or Bert Schneider who produced the movie. Don't call me. I directed the film, you know."

So that started it and he had a lot of time to work on his excuse for having written this movie. And then he convinced his son (which is really pathetic to me) that he had written it. This has become a big, big thing with things printed in the New Yorker and all over the place. And it really hurts me. It's one of my really, really prize things that I've done. It has nothing to do with Terry Southern. Absolutely nothing, except the title Easy Rider.

And that's just the way it is, man and it's such a thorn in my side...

MC: Did you not try to challenge him legally or something before he died?

DH: No, he died before I could do that. But I was in the court situation, unfortunately, with Rip Torn.

MC: Oh yes. You lost big time on that, didn't you...

DH: I lost money because they all came in and then testified against me.

MC: You said this thing, "I am responsible for cocaine taking in the US." What did you mean by that?

DH: Well, at the beginning, Peter had it as marijuana and I said, "We can't, carry enough marijuana in dirt bikes to go anywhere man." Then people suggested heroin and I said, "That's not a great idea. No, man, I don't want us promoting heroin." I said, "What about cocaine? You know, cocaine's the drug of kings." I'd only seen it a couple of times. Count Basie, Duke Ellington, a few of the big bands had some around, but it was never on the street and it was never anything. I'd read that Freud had used it and I thought this must be harmless stuff so why don't we just use it? In 1969 the movie came out. By 1971 cocaine was everywhere on the street. It was the most prevalent drug in the United States suddenly. So that's what I meant when I said, "Unfortunately that opened up the cocaine market." Because it wasn't there before.

MC: So you must regret that.

DH: I can't regret anything that happened. I mean... it's not about regretting really. It's about... it's an unfortunate thing that happened. I mean, I still like the movie.

The killing of Lady
Macduff's son in
<u>Macbeth</u> (1971)
Roman Polanski (Director)

p.96

The ending of
<u>Fat</u> <u>City</u> (1972)
Jeff Bridges (Actor)

p.100

Brando's wife dies in
<u>Last</u> <u>Tango</u> <u>in</u> <u>Paris</u> (1972)
Bernardo Bertolucci (Director)

p.102

The "Don't Sell Me
America" scene in
<u>Save</u> <u>the</u> <u>Tiger</u> (1973)
Jack Lemmon (Actor)

p.110

On the shooting of Billy in
<u>Pat</u> <u>Garrett</u> <u>and</u> <u>Billy</u> <u>the</u> <u>Kid</u>
(1973)
James Coburn (Actor)

p.114

Politics and the
bread making scene in
<u>The</u> <u>Shootist</u> (1976)
Lauren Bacall (Actress)

p.124

The sex scene in
<u>Fellini's</u> <u>Casanova</u> (1976)
Donald Sutherland (Actor)

p.126

1

2

3

4

5

6

21ST SEPTEMBER 2000, THE
CHATEAU MARMONT HOTEL,
SUNSET BOULEVARD

[At a wrap party at the end of filming
a Western in a small Mexican town,
Kansas, a movie extra and stuntman
(Hopper) becomes emotional. A single
shot follows him out of a room, into
the night where he stops and cries
(Figs.1-5). In a parallel story in the
film, Hopper also plays the director
of the Western.] (Fig.6)

MARK COUSINS: What are your
thoughts about that scene?

DENNIS HOPPER: Well first of all,
James Dean came to me on Giant.
We were in a restaurant, he called me
over to his table and he said, "I saw
you do a scene today and I thought
you were really great in it." It was a
scene where I have a verbal fight with
Rock Hudson because I've married a
Mexican girl and I'm going off to try
to help some people who've had been
injured in a hurricane... He said,
"Barrymore would be very proud, if
he could have seen you." He listed a
group of actors that he knew and that
I admired and said, "I wish they could
have been here today and... you were
playing moment-to-moment reality
very well and I think it's a great step
forward." So I dropped a little tear out
of my eye and he said, "You see that
tear? I know what that means. That
means you appreciate what I'm telling
you. You know when you really have
to cry, you have to leave the room.
It's not something you share with
somebody." And he said, "To do that

in the movie, to be able to achieve in
the movie, that would be something."
So that little scene in my mind is a
sort of homage to James Dean.

The killing of Lady
Macduff's son in
Macbeth (1971)
Roman Polanski (Director)

p.97

6TH MARCH 2000, LA SALLE DES
FETES, MUSEE D'ORSAY, PARIS

MARK COUSINS: You were born in
Paris, you were brought up in Krakow,
and you of course lived through the
Krakow ghetto (Fig.8). Do those
experiences seem a long time ago
now, or are they often in your mind?

ROMAN POLANSKI: They're more
in my mind recently than before, for
several reasons. One of them is that
I have children now and I... relate
to these events through their eyes,
somehow, and also through the
imaginary eyes of my parents... I
know now how my parents felt about
me running away, when they were
being taken to the concentration
camps. Now, being a parent, I know
what separation from a child means.
I know how tragic it is. Now I know
also what it means for the parents,
when the child is torn away. I always
knew that I was going to make a film
in Poland, a film somehow related
to the history of those days and now
I think it is the time to do this and
that's why I decided to acquire the
rights to the book which was quite
successful in England, a book called,
The Pianist (by Wladyslaw Szpilman)
which relates the survival of a
musician in the Warsaw ghetto.

MC: And so, if you have had in your
mind for a long time the idea of
making a film about those days, why
did you not accept Steven Spielberg's
offer to direct Schindler's List (1993)?

RP: Schindler's List... was really
about the Krakow ghetto, that's
where I was. To do a film about that
particular ghetto and the people who
went with Schindler, it's too close...
on one hand and too far on the other.
Too close, because it deals with the
days and with things, walls, streets
that I know intimately and too far,
because it deals with this group of
people who were saved by working
for Schindler. If I was to go through
the pain of recreating it all, I would
rather do something with my own
childhood, my own persona and the
people around me.

MC: And in the ghetto you saw
people shot. You say in your memoir
(Roman), you saw German propaganda
films where it said that Jews were
equated to lice and rats. To what
extent did these damage you, or
make you feel inferior?

RP: Not at all.

MC: Why not?

RP: Well, why would it?

MC: Because if you're bombarded
with these images, if you're made
to live in a way that is sub-human
compared to the people outside the
ghetto, surely, unless you're a very
mature person, you would begin to
take things on board...

RP: There are millions of people who
are living in sub-human conditions
right now and they're not all going
to be all screwed up by it. There are

30TH APRIL 2001, FOUR SEASONS
RESORT, SANTA BARBARA

MARK COUSINS: You made a film
with a director who was very much
from old Hollywood, John Huston.
How good do you think <u>Fat City</u> is?

JEFF BRIDGES: Oh, it's a wonderful
film. A lot of great memories making
that movie.

MC: Somebody should make a new
print and re-release it.

JB: Yeah. That would be a good idea.

MC: Huston's recent films hadn't
been all that good. <u>Fat City</u> was set in
Stockton which had then the highest
unemployment in the US. You play a
boxer on the way up and Stacy Keach
plays a boxer on the way down and
the twist is that because you are
white, you are novelty acts, the
non-whites will pay more to see you
box. I've got here the last scene of
the film, do you remember that...?

JB: Oh, very well...

[Night. Boxers Ernie Munger (Bridges)
and Billy Tully (Keach) walk into a
grim, brightly lit cafe. They sit at the
bar. Time passes. They look at the old
Philippino man serving them.]
(Figs.1-3)

ERNIE: <u>Maybe</u> <u>he's</u> <u>happy?</u>
BILLY: <u>Maybe</u> <u>we're</u> <u>all</u> <u>happy.</u>

JB: There's an interesting story about
this scene... John Huston was feeling
really quite bad when we were doing
that film and would have an oxygen
tank next to him. We shot this
scene towards the end of the film.
It was about 3.30 in the morning or
something like that, they were setting
up and John was in his director's
chair with his bottle of oxygen. We
didn't know if he was asleep or maybe
he was dead. We didn't know. And
nobody had the guts to go over and
shake him because they were afraid
he was just going to go over.

[Ernie and Billy continue to drink
their coffee. Then Billy turns around
and looks at the rest of the room.
Freeze, optical move closer to his face,
then cut to the bar where the people
smoking, playing cards and walking
around all come to a halt.] (Figs.4-6)

So we were waiting for him to wake up
and they were all ready and then he
went, "Oh, I've got it!" (Figs.7-8) And
everybody gathered around. He said,
"Have you ever been to a party, when
all of a sudden, for no apparent reason,
everybody just stops what they're
doing? You've had that experience,
haven't you? Well that's what I want
to happen. Stacy, when you turn
around, I want everybody to just stop."
He just wanted to get this strange
sense of the universe stopping. One of
the assistant directors or something
said, "Well John we can just freeze
frame." And he said, "No, no, no... I
want the people to stop and I want the
smoke to continue..." (Fig.9)

MC: And the sound disappears...

JB: Yeah... and as I'm looking at
it, it looks as if they did freeze the
frame, but the people were directed
just to stop... but I was watching
the cigarettes there and the cigarette
smoke stops too. That wasn't his
original intention.

MC: Why is the film so good?

JB: Well it, it broke a lot of rules. I
remember Conrad Hall, the guy who
shot it, was getting so much flak from
the execs and Ray Stark because they
couldn't see what was happening,
but Connie intentionally did that.
He wanted it to be like when you go
into a bar, you've just come from the
bright light and your eyes haven't
adjusted yet, it all looks too dark and
you go outside and it blows out. Well
the whole film is shot like that and
Connie got very close to being fired
and John said, "No, this is the way
we want it." And that was very against
the way film was being shot in those
days. And now it doesn't look very
surprising because everybody ripped
them off.

That's one reason. Also you've
got great performances. Stacy was
wonderful. Susan Tyrrell did a great
job and John really loved boxing
very much.

1

2   3

1ST DECEMBER 1998,
A LONDON STUDIO

MARK COUSINS: You once said that Last Tango in Paris was like a documentary, like a Jean Rouch movie about Marlon Brando. Do you remember that scene where Schneider is asking him to talk about himself and Brando says things about his childhood, about standing in cow shit?... And these are things really from Brando's life. You haven't continued to use that "vérité" documentary approach to things, why?

BERNARDO BERTOLUCCI: The only way I can shoot a movie is, as Jean Renoir said, "to let the door open and let the unpredictable reality come into the shot, come into the movie."

[Medium close-up of Marlon Brando (as the widower, Paul) lying on the floor.] (Fig.1)

PAUL: I remember one time when I was all dressed up to go out and take this girl to a basketball game and I started to go out and my father said, "You have to milk the cow" and I asked him, I said, "Would you please milk the cow?" and he says, "No, get your arse out there." I went out and I was in a hurry, I didn't have time to change my shoes and had cow shit all over my shoes on the way to the basketball game, it smelled in the car.

BB: You know, if Marlon arrived with a devastated face, because he had a very naughty night... Instead of putting a lot of make up on his face, I used this devastated face, because that was in front of the camera and there is no make-up that can hide the truth from the camera... So that was my deal with Marlon Brando. I didn't want the same Marlon, the fantastic Marlon we have seen in On the Waterfront and Viva Zapata! (1952). I said to Marlon, I want to get out of your face, take off... the Actors Studio, Stanislavski, the Strasberg mask. He never answered, yes or no. Then seeing the movie I thought, I've succeeded. Marlon Brando in Last Tango is much closer to what Marlon is in life.

And then two or three years ago, I had a long meeting with Marlon. After a long time, I told him, "Don't you think that I achieved my mission to take off the mask?" Marlon said, he had this little smile, "You think that one was me, ha ha!"

But in fact, it has always been my way of approaching a story, to use the camera as if I was doing a documentary. You said, "cinéma vérité" which is very right.

There was a monologue of Marlon's character in front of the corpse of his dead wife and it was coming very much from a Strindberg text, I never told Marlon that. It had a kind of a misogynist drive and Marlon changed it, started to come out with this very emotional thing, "You big fucker, tell me the truth et cetera, et cetera, et cetera." And Marlon doesn't like to learn dialogue by heart, the dialogue is written just behind the camera. He likes to look for a second, catch a word of the dialogue, (Fig.2) from that word reconstruct in his memory what he has to say... and he's there looking at the dead wife and there's a huge blackboard with all the dialogue written...

(laughing) It's nice to reveal this!

[A distraught Paul sits beside and then climbs on the body of his dead wife, which is laid out surrounded by flowers. (Fig.3) Occasionally, as he talks, he glances to a board offscreen...]

PAUL: Come on, tell me you didn't lie. Haven't you got anything to say about that, you can think of something can't you? Tell me something, go on smile you cunt... Go on tell me something sweet, smile at me and say I just misunderstood. Go on, tell me you pig fucker, you god damn fucking pig, fucking liar. Rosa, I'm sorry, I, I just can't, I can't stand it... to see the goddamned look on your face...

BB: Marlon is famous for that. I remember he was so happy when Maria Schneider was giving him the line just next to the camera and she would appear in front of him (he was in a close-up) with the dialogue written on her forehead. He would be so happy, because we were making fun of him and he has a good sense of humour...

1

2

3

4

5

6

7

8

9

10

11

12

13

14

15

The death of a child,
the scaffolding collapse
and the sex scene in
Don't Look Now (1973)
Donald Sutherland (Actor)

p.105

18TH OCTOBER 2000, CENTURY PLAZA HOTEL, CENTURY CITY, LOS ANGELES

MARK COUSINS: You made two very different films about the death of a child, Don't Look Now and Ordinary People (1980). Near the beginning of Don't Look Now, you have a premonition that your daughter is dying. It's one of the most memorable scenes in cinema.

[John Baxter (Sutherland) stands over a light box studying a slide of a church interior. His head slowly rises. Cut to his son running. Back to John moving towards the door as his wife, Laura (Julie Christie) asks, "What's the matter?" He blankly replies "Nothing." Cut to his young daughter plunging, in slow motion, deep into a large garden pond. John runs through the garden, straight to the pond in an attempt to rescue her.] (Figs.1-2)

(Sutherland looks away from the screen, distressed by it.)

Finding it hard to look at this?

DONALD SUTHERLAND: Yes, it is, yes... (Figs.3-6)

[Cut back to the slide. A red figure now sits in the church interior. Liquid spills. The red figure seems to bleed.]

DS: Oh God...

[John rises from the water with his dead daughter in his arms and lets out a cry.] (Figs.7-9)

MC: It's shocking isn't it? It's not in the novella (by Daphne Du Maurier), this scene.

DS: Oh God. He is brilliant, Nic Roeg, absolutely brilliant. One of the great directors, because of the way he edits, the way he lights, the way he sees things. Often he has gone askew, but in that particular picture, we would have done anything for him. We dubbed as much of the picture as we could, because Nic and I thought and I seemed in some way to be willing, that I would die in the process of it. So much were we committed, we were so fatalistic about the way the production was going. You see, sometimes in our business, you have strong, sometimes profound intellectual, emotional... relationships, then it's over. (Fig.15)

MC: Back to the fatalism in Don't Look Now.

DS: Well, the scene where I dangle from a rope in there, that is real, that's me.

[John is restoring mosaic high up in a Venetian church. A plank falls from the scaffolding. Then nothing. It plunges through a glass panel and knocks John off his hoist, causing havoc as his work material plunges to the ground. He clings to a rope, swinging.] (Figs.10-13)

DS: I have vertigo and this scene cured it. A stunt man said, "The insurance is wrong, you are hanging fifty feet above a marble floor, you fall, you're dead." He said, "I'm not

going to do it", and Nic said, "What are we going to do, we have this church for one day." I said, "I'll do it, I'll do it, I'll do it." So I climb up the darn thing. I've got a harness on with a curbing wire, we attach the curbing wire to the rope, up through my sleeve, we throw a two by ten at me, hit me in the back, the thing falls apart, I drop down, I am on the curbing wire. Nic has told me, "You are just going to drop down, we will pull you right in." So I drop down. Nic is so excited by the fact that he has got this actor hanging fifty feet up in the air, he's got two guys with sticks, pushing me. I am swirling like that, (twirls his hand) (Fig.14) in the middle of the thing. I saw Victor Armstrong (Raiders of the Lost Ark, 1981, Tomorrow Never Dies, 1997), who is one of the great stunt co-ordinators, a couple of years later, and he said, "That was a brave thing." I said, "Was nothing, really. I had a curbing wire", he said, "You had a curbing wire?" I said, "Yeah." He said, "But you were spinning." I said, "Yeah." He said, "Well when you spin like that with a curbing wire, the curbing wire snaps." I was... you know... but it was like that, the whole picture was like that. It was an extraordinary experience, so much so, that Francine and I named our first born, after Nic.

MC: The day after you did the vertigo shot, you did the famous sex scene.

DS: ...Let's talk about it before you look. It's obvious these are two people, who in real life don't know each other, and who aren't doing anything. He cut it together in such a way that none of it is voyeuristic, yet it just reminds you of having made love yourself, the times in your own past, some wonderful love affair that you have had. He didn't stay on the lovers. You were there when they were getting dressed and it is intercut like that all the time... and that saved it. The only reason why it's good is because it lives in people's memory, as opposed to being something you watch and think, "Oh God."

[A hotel room in wintry Venice. John and Laura are lying on a bed looking at magazines. They start to make love. It is perhaps the first time they've done so since the death of their child. Piano music begins, gradual at first but building. Cut to them getting dressed and then cut back to the love-making. The actors are constantly changing positions, the camera is never static. The dressing actions sometimes match the love-making ones.] (Figs.16-19)

MC: Roeg once said that his intention was to give the impression that she becomes pregnant during this scene... and look at those matches of dressing and undressing, is it heavily directed?

DS: Heavily directed. All the way through that we were just alone in the room with Nic and Tony Richmond (director of photography) with two unblimped Arriflexes and Nic is saying (brrrr, mimicking noise of camera), "I like that" (brrrr), and "Alright, Donald put your mouth on Julie's breast" (brrrr), "Alright, Julie,

come" (brrrr), it was like that. [The scene continues.]

MC: It shows, it's not just accidental cuts.

DS: No, nothing with Nic is accidental, nothing. It's all in his imagination and he fuses it on the film. No, no, every position he told us to go and do.

[The love-making becomes more passionate.]

MC: You knew that M*A*S*H (1970) was going to be something special, did you know that this was going to be too?

DS: No, I only knew that I was extraordinarily proud of it.

[Laura twists her body. Cut, and she's clothed. Her heads turns to camera.]

MC: Wasn't that gorgeous the way she turns round like that?

DS: I thought it was me! I'm so skinny... God. Look at her...

MC: Is it not great to be an actor? You can look back at scenes like this, not even for the erotic content, but because of great times.

DS: Yeah, but can I tell you something, the abiding thing, when you are looking back on it, is, "Oh, the wig looks good", because I was always wearing a curly wig, just clipped in here. When I would finish, I would unclip it, pull it off. We were working

in hotels all the time and so people would see me standing there and I would just go, "click" like that and then they'd go "Ahh!"

MC: But in the scenes we've looked at, you are not only responding to things like "the wig looks good", you've been touched by them too, so you can stand back enough to respond to them emotionally...

DS: Well what can be worse, I don't even dare talk about it, losing a child. I don't know how people survive that. And as far as emotion goes Joseph Brodsky, the Russian poet, gave a commencement lecture at Dartmouth University and he talked to all those graduating students and he said, "Today is the best day of your life. From now on, it's going to get boring and more boring, the more goods you acquire, the more money you have, it's just going to make it more boring." Then he cautioned them and said, "Try to stay passionate, leave the cool to the constellations, passion alone is a remedy against boredom and that has been the driving force in my life, passion." The pursuit of whatever truthfulness you can find in acting, giving that to a director and hoping that he will take those pieces and use it for the benefit of this film.

Overleaf: Julie Christie, Donald Sutherland and Nicolas Roeg between takes in Don't Look Now (1973).

16

17

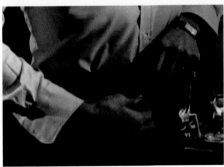

18

19

6TH MAY 1998, BEVERLY HILTON,
LOS ANGELES

MARK COUSINS: In the early 70s,
you made Save the Tiger. On the way
home from the set or location, you
would cry in the car. Why did you cry?

JACK LEMMON: It was one of those
things that actors have to be careful
of. The part began to take me over
instead of me controlling the part. In
Save the Tiger, the guy was walking
around having a nervous breakdown.

And the scenes began to get to me and
I didn't realise the extent to which I
was involved. So, as a result, I started
cracking up on the way home from
and driving to work. Then about the
third morning, when I was sobbing
like a baby while driving down the
freeway, a cop pulled me over and
he recognised me and he said, "Are
you okay, Mr Lemmon?" And I said,
"Yeah, I'm sorry I don't know why. I
was thinking about a scene that we're
going to do." He said, "Well, I'm going
to follow you to make sure you're
okay. Just drive slowly and try to
keep control of yourself." So I said,
"Okay." He followed me to the Biltmore
hotel. I realised then that I was
beginning to behave like the character.
Once I realised that, it never happened
again. It's the only time that's
happened to me. (Figs.4-6)

MC: And you got your second Oscar
for this film. There's one scene in it
where your character decries the fact
that the younger generation doesn't
know who Goebbels is, doesn't

history. Now earlier today, you told
me that in your youth you weren't
politicised, you weren't into these
matters and slowly through meeting
Felicia (Lemmon's wife), you became
interested in history and politics.

JL: I think I was somewhat aware
but not in any way nearly as much
as I've become.

MC: Is it true that when you toured
with Billy Wilder in Europe,
publicising The Apartment (1960),
you went to Berlin and Wilder hadn't
told you until then that his family
had died in the Holocaust?

JL: Yeah, I took a little walk with him
one afternoon. We got out of the car
at one place, and it was like a series
of brownstones. Each house we
passed, all you could see was bullet
marks, in the sides of the buildings
and the fronts like the building had
measles. And he stopped in front of
one and looked up, then he got very
teary. I said, "What's wrong Billy?"
And he said, "We lived there."

(Lemmon pauses for moment, moved.)

[Harry Stoner (Lemmon) and rag
trade business partner Phil Greene
(Jack Gilford) discuss the financial
problems of their business. Stoner
suggests torching the factory but
Greene does not agree.]

GREENE: Don't you understand? It's
people like us, people in the middle,
that made this country work. And
when people like ourselves get into

this kind of thing... it takes it all down... that's what's tearing this country apart.
STONER: (hysterical) Stop it, you son of a bitch! Don't sell America to me. I've got friends over there sitting under the sand with bikinis on their heads. (Fig.7)

[Stoner pauses and calms down.]

I used to get goose bumps every time I looked at that flag. When I was a kid sitting alone in the room, playing the radio, if they played the national anthem, I stood up. All alone in the room, I stood up to attention. Don't sell me America. Now they're making jock straps out of the flag! (Figs.1-3)

JL: That was the first script that Steve Shagan wrote.

MC: And apparently he begged you to play it.

JL: Yeah, it's actually kind of funny. I was doing a CBS film. This fellow came on set and introduced himself. He said, "I've got a script that I've written with you in mind that I hope you like and I'd really appreciate it if you'd read it." I said, "Sure", what was I going to say? So he handed it to me. He left and I threw it in my little dressing room trailer on set and it sat there for a couple of days, while I did my work. I didn't start it because it said Save the Tiger and I couldn't see me swinging through the trees going "Aaaoooooowwww!", like some kind of old Tarzan. Anyhow, finally, with

nothing to do between scenes, with a long wait, I sat down and I opened it up and I started to read it. By page three I was hooked, and I just went crazy for it. So I got a hold of him right away and I said, "I've almost finished this script and I can only tell you, I'm dying to do it." He said terrific and that was the start of that.

MC: And it's called, Save the Tiger, because tigers always return to places of remembered beauty. What was Harry Stoner's remembered beauty?

JL: I think that the only releases he had, were his reminiscences and remembrances of the old days that he loved, the old songs, the beachhead during the war and his comradeship from the war days. Days of baseball when he was a kid when he'd watch the Yankees and the Dodgers. I think that he was an idealistic young man. It just is an example of how good men can do indecent things. He lost the whole damn thing, it's the misuse of the American dream so to speak, which is misused all the time because it becomes so material. A pool, a Cadillac, the right school for the kids, enough money for the servants, all of this jazz and everything becomes more important than anything else, which is too bad because there are things that are important.

But to Harry, his life is really summed up in my favourite lines in the entire film. It's only two words. One night in the clothes factory, he's walking around and an old tailor is still working there. The old tailor looks

at him when he sits down to talk to him for a minute and says, "Harry, what do you want in life, what is it, what do you want?" And he thinks for a few seconds and then says, "Another season", meaning another season of clothes to sell. That's it, unfortunately and I think Harry knows it's wrong too, but he can't help it, that's what he has become.

7

20TH AUGUST 1999, L'ERMITAGE HOTEL, BEVERLY HILLS

MARK COUSINS: The 1970s was your best decade in a way, because of your collaboration with Sam Peckinpah (Fig.10). Why is he an important film-maker?

JAMES COBURN: Well, he was one of the most important film-makers at that particular time because he was a unique human being. He also was a renegade, an outcast. He was a drunk. He had all of these things going against him. He hated every producer he ever worked with. He put them all on notice that if they ever came on set he would stop shooting.

It was amazing, most of those guys would say, "Let's get Peckinpah to do the film, and I can handle him." And none of them could handle him. He didn't need handling. All they had to do was turn him loose and he would make a brilliant film. Most of the films were taken away from him, especially in the cutting room. Pat Garrett and Billy the Kid was. He made a brilliant film. The director's cut still exists in Samoa. There's a guy up there who handles all Peckinpah's archives. And that's the only real director's cut. There's another so-called one, but it's actually the television cut.

It's really a shame because he had an extraordinary sense of reality and of dynamics. Talk about violence, well I guess you can call it violence, but we called it action then. We made a lot of action movies because that's what was demanded. That was the trip, from Major Dundee (1965), Pat Garrett and Billy the Kid to The Wild Bunch (1969). The Ballad of Cable Hogue (1970) was probably one of the most sensitive films that he made. It was just a shame he didn't get the chance to make more films. He called himself a working alcoholic and he was.

I got him off the liquor and immediately he started snorting cocaine! What a guy! I loved him, man. He was just a lot of fun to be around and you never knew what was going to happen. He gave medals for anybody who finished movies with him. Everybody, the crew and all the actors, got a medal, if they finished a movie. But there were a lot of them that didn't finish.

MC: Had he an optimistic view of human beings?

JC: I think everybody but producers. When they came on set he would stop shooting immediately and say, "Get him off, off, off. Get Off!" And this naturally didn't ingratiate him too much to the people who were making the movies. He'd always say, "Marty", Marty Blom was his agent, "Get me final cut." And so Marty would say, "You got final cut, Sam." And he never had it.

MC: You say he was an optimist, except for producers. But, when you look at his films, what they say is that people, left to their own devices, turn to violence.

to the ground. (Figs.2-3) The shots cut between Billy falling and the onlookers reacting. Garrett catches a glimpse of his own refection in a mirror and shoots. The glass shatters into pieces.] (Figs.4-6)

MC: Peckinpah would do that to himself, sit in bed and shoot himself in the mirror. Did you ever see that?

JC: Yeah, but I think it was because he was shooting something else and he missed! On weekends he'd spend most of the time in bed and get drunk on vodka or whatever it was... I think one time he missed and hit the mirror. But I don't think he would ever do it consciously because he didn't hate himself.

And no one hated him, none of the actors hated Sam. They loved working with him because it always brought out the best in them. He would demand more from everybody on the crew. He was the hardest director I ever worked with. Most of the time it's so easy, just say the lines. He wouldn't allow that to happen. He wouldn't allow the prop man to come on set unless he had three or four choices. "What do you mean you've only got one of them? Goddammit! Out! Off the set! Get off! Get rid of this guy!"

Sam really got pretty weird at the end and lost all of his friends. He just got over the edge and nobody would work with him. I wouldn't work with him. He invited me down to see a rough cut of The Osterman Weekend (1983),

his last film. He was trying to get enough money to edit the final reel. He had this cane and was limping. He said, "Listen, I don't know what it is here but they won't give me enough money to finish the film now." So we listened and watched the film and the producers were there. And they were a bunch of bean counters. Everything worked really good, it was nice, smooth up till the final reel and then it just... All it needed was fine tuning, bringing together. So we finished and they said, "So what do you think Mr Coburn? What do you think about that movie?" I said, "It's great up until the final reel. What happened there? What have you done?" He said, "They won't give me enough money, blah, blah, blah!"

MC: Alan Sharp, who wrote The Osterman Weekend, once said that some Sam Peckinpah pictures are like adverts for the NRA, the National Rifle Association.

JC: No, no they're not. They're the absolute antithesis of that. I mean if you look at a Sam Peckinpah film, you don't want to go shoot anybody. He was not a violent man. He hated violence. He couldn't stand up to anybody because he was usually too loaded, but he'd hope that somebody would stop him.

7

8

9

10

25TH MARCH 1998, SCORSESE'S
OFFICE, PARK AVENUE, NEW YORK

MARK COUSINS: <u>Mean</u> <u>Streets</u>
made you a star, didn't it? Your
phone started ringing all the time,
you got lots of scripts offered to you.

MARTIN SCORSESE: That's what
they tell me, yeah.

MC: Did you want to be famous?

MS: Oh yeah, absolutely, yes.

MC: And did that whole generation
you met then? Spielberg, Schrader…

MS: Yeah, we all did. When I was
at NYU, I knew I was a director.
I made a living editing somewhat,
mainly other people's films and
documentaries. I was also making
a living doing a little bit of writing.
But basically the only thing I really
can't do on my own and I've tried,
is lighting. I have no knowledge of
lighting or how a camera works.
I've done 16mm and things like that,
but where I come from, it was always
dark. (laughs)

MC: So, do you always leave it to
your director of photography?

MS: Pretty much. Well no, I design
with him. I design the shots, the
movements of the shots and the size
of the frame. I have a real problem,
sometimes, dealing with the light. I
don't know where it's coming from.
It's New York! I mean look at us
right now. Just turn the light on.

Do you want the sun shining through
here? That's absurd. Don't tell me
you want smoke in the light too. That
doesn't happen in my office or the
editing room. Put a constant light
on, what do I care? (Figs.4-6)

But despite this, I felt I was a director.
I thought I was, even when other
people didn't take me very seriously.
I was shameless! I went to every
party in LA and I promoted myself,
shamelessly! Dreadful! Horrible!

MC: As a working class person,
where did you get this confidence?

MS: Oh, I was working class, but I
never worked. My parents worked.
They gave me the money to go to
school, I had asthma, was taken
care of. I was a crazy film-maker,
I wanted to make movies!

MC: But there's this issue of
confidence. Working class people
often don't have it.

MS: I don't know why, you're right.
I have no idea. I was burnt with the
passion of these moving images and
emotions that I saw growing up
around me and had to combine the
two. I don't know how else to do it!

[Charlie (Harvey Keitel) walks into
a sleazy bar. The handheld camera
follows as he greets the barman and
his friend Tony (David Proval).]

<u>CHARLIE:</u> <u>I've</u> <u>come</u> <u>to</u> <u>create</u> <u>order.
Carl, JB and Soda please.</u> (Fig.1)

[The barman places the glass in front of him.] (Fig.2)

CHARLIE: May God be with you.

MS: Well that's the first chapter of Ulysses.

TONY: Let me ask you something. Are thou the king of the Jews? (Fig.3)
CHARLIE: Does thou sayest to thyself or have others told in me?
TONY: Am I a Jew?
CHARLIE: I came unto this world.

MC: So, you had read James Joyce at the time you were making Mean Streets?

MS: Yeah, I didn't understand it, I identified more with Portrait of an Artist and Dubliners. But, where we sat around, quotes from the Scriptures came out all the time. People spoke that way. Not necessarily as clearly as in this scene, but the saints were called upon. I'll never forget one woman, who was a friend, said, "I'm never praying to the Virgin Mary anymore, I'm sick of praying to her. I've prayed to her for this favour a thousand times and it's not happened. I refuse to pray." My friend and I said, "Well, that will show the Virgin Mary! That will show her!" (laughs)

That was all very real, this is part of it. In the film it goes off into the deep end but I mean it all has to do with seeing a lot of Italian films. It is Italian. In Pasolini's Accattone (1961), there's an incredible scene, when Accattone decides to stop being a pimp. One character says to him, "Today you'll sell your watch, tomorrow you'll sell your gold chain and in a week you'll not have the eyes to cry with." It's poetry, "I say unto you", it's like the Bible, "You'll have no eyes to cry with." And that's what I heard growing up. I don't understand a lot of it, especially Ulysses, but then you do get to understand it. I've got a little reader's guide and am getting through it a second time now. But there's no doubt that the reverence of Buck Mulligan has a lot to do with this scene. Not just reverence, a lot of it is irreverent about religion too; cursing God and the saints about the situation we're in. For the people on the streets, it was a constant thing, it was very alive.

MC: And James Joyce's idea of escaping the "net of religion" as he put it. Is that what your characters are trying to do, escape the neighbourhood?

MS: Yeah.

MC: I've got another scene here from Mean Streets. How did you do it?

[Charlie, after a long drinking binge, continues to mingle with friends at the party. The camera faces him, equidistant, framing his bloated face. The background moves within the frame, but he doesn't. He jolts and staggers towards the door, creating a nauseous sensation. Acquaintances drunkenly greet and embrace him.] (Fig.7)

MS: He had a body brace underneath his jacket for the Arriflex camera. We put a board at the end of it and put a camera at the end of the board. There was a guy walking backwards because the board would bounce.

[Charlie becomes queasy and slowly, in several stages, falls to the ground.]

And finally when he got on the ground, we went sideways with him. See! Just like a ballet dancer, he eased himself down, sideways.

MC: I think it's the best drunk scene in the movies.

MS: That's what it felt like, some of those nights...

7

1

2

3

8TH MAY 2000, AT A NEW YORK ART GALLERY

MARK COUSINS: In 1976 you made The Shootist about an old gunslinger (John Wayne) who's dying of cancer, and in real life Wayne...

LAUREN BACALL: ...he was dying of cancer.

MC: I've got here the scene in The Shootist where you play a landlady and he comes to stay. It's the end of an era, 1901. Queen Victoria has died. The world is changing. He's from the old world and then this happens...

[The scene opens as widow Bond Rogers (Bacall) is in the kitchen making bread. Legendary gunfighter John B. Books (Wayne) enters and apologises for misleading his landlady into believing he is a respectable man.] (Fig.1)

LB: (watching) He was very good in this movie.

[Mrs Rogers asks him to leave her house as the damage is done.]

MRS ROGERS: Rubbish! You lied to me, you made a fool of me and you took advantage of me. This house is all I have and if my lodgers find out who you are, they'll leave and... (Fig.2)

BOOKS: I have a cancer.

[The widow stops, shocked and lost for words.]

BOOKS: I'm dying of it.

LB: That'll stop you, won't it.

MC: Actors often say that one of the hardest things to do is surprise. When he says, "I have a cancer", your surprise is good. When you're in a scene like that and you know he's going to say, "I have a cancer", how do you make it fresh?

LB: Well, you have to play these scenes as though you've never heard it before. As though you didn't know. It's one of the disciplines of acting. Whether it's on screen or on stage, you have to psyche yourself into the idea – this is the first time I've ever said these words. And so your reactions must be fresh. Especially on film, because that camera sees everything. (Fig.3)

MC: Wayne was famously a conservative, and you were the other side of the fence. So, was your relationship fractious?

LB: Not at all. We never discussed anything political. I remember when we were making Blood Alley (1955).

MC: ...Your first film together.

LB: Yeah. And we were living in some motel for a few days. We were on location. I remember I was in bed and I heard him coming home at night with a couple of his friends, drunk as a skunk. Talking about Roosevelt... bah Roosevelt... Did he hate Roosevelt! And I thought, "Oh God please let that never come up while I'm around." And it never did. And Duke and I, it is the fascinating thing about life, we not only got along well but we were attracted to one another. Now you go figure it out. You can't.

MC: You once said that he was gentle, which is not how we think of John Wayne, this very tough man, like a rock.

LB: Yes. When he drank all of his frustrations and anger came out and of course, he fought. But other than that... he was very, very right wing (she rolls her eyes), God knows. And his friends were very right wing (she rolls them more). But he was great to work with. Of course he liked to direct you. He'd take you and say, "Now you go over here and I go..." But we really got along incredibly well. The chemistry was really good.

18TH OCTOBER 2000, CENTURY PLAZA HOTEL, CENTURY CITY, LOS ANGELES

MARK COUSINS: Here's an extract from a filmed interview with a director you might recognise – Mr Fellini.

[Fellini interview: Since I've never seen a Donald Sutherland film...]

MC: (pausing tape) "Since I had never seen a Donald Sutherland film!" He had been in a film with you (Alex in Wonderland, 1970, directed by Paul Mazursky)...

DONALD SUTHERLAND: Well, yes of course (laughs). He was lying through his teeth. He had never seen a Donald Sutherland movie...

[The interview resumes: ...only his photograph. I decided on him because he was so far from the conventional stereotype of Casanova, the seducer, the Latin lover and then attempting to make him as similar as possible to portraits of Casanova. I acted a little sadism to change his face...]

MC: (pausing) "A little sadism"...

DS: He changed my nose, my chin, my eyebrows and my head. Cut my hair back here. I thought I looked beautiful... God I loved him. It's so nice to see him. (Figs.1-2)

FELLINI: I gave him a false chin, a false nose and I shaved off half his hair. So Sutherland was slightly alarmed, a little intimidated, but I tried to make him understand that my project had nothing to do with the illustration of Casanova's memoirs, but that it was quite different. He was a puppet, not a man, engrossed in his mechanical sexual act.

DS: See, that scene that he is talking about changed his idea of the film, because when he saw the two of us, Adela Lojodice, the wonderful actress who played the doll in this, it changed his whole perception of how the rest of the film should go.

MC: Here is the scene.

[Sutherland is in bed embracing a life-sized, mechanical doll dressed up in nineteenth century fashion. He pulls the doll onto himself and starts to have sex with her. (Fig.3) In close-up we see her blank face. Her head turns slightly, her eyes flicker. (Fig.6) Sutherland starts to cry out, "I love you, I love you." (Fig.4) When he has finished, he places the doll beside him. Suddenly her leg shoots up.]

DS: Look at it. This is a wonderful... (Fig.5)

MC: The complete opposite to the sex scene with you and Julie Christie isn't it? One is totally organic, one is totally inorganic. Why did that scene change Fellini's conception of the film?

MC: Oh, because suddenly when Casanova started saying, "I love you", it gave him access to the character of Casanova that he hadn't had before.

The onanistic access, the need for love, the constant recreation of himself in the pursuit of love. Total narcissism, where things begin again with no history, no past. So what Fellini had been doing, which was for him a little superficial in design, a little caricatured, suddenly moved into an area of reality. And he followed that right through to the dance on the ice at the end, which was not a part of the picture until he created this scene.

MC: Fellini says of Casanova, "He is a turd of a man" whereas you seem to have more sympathy with him. That would make for a collision...

DS: No, there is no collision, I am playing the character, therefore I love the character. It's not possible to play a character that you hate, you cannot do that. Of course, if you look at all the books... Pepys or Boswell; I guess it was Boswell called him "New House". And there are very few references to Casanova in historical documents. He wrote a lot but was inconsequential, and yet, he thought of himself as someone significant. And Federico thought of him as a fraud. He thought that he truly represented Roman life. I think the film is very beautiful. He showed it to me with great pride and he said, "This picture will allow me to work in the United States", and then Pauline Kael (the New Yorker film critic) killed it, just killed it, because that was the year they didn't like European films.

1   2   3

4   5   6

7   8   9

4TH FEBRUARY 1998, A LOFT IN
LOWER MANHATTAN

PAUL SCHRADER: (The script) was
written as therapy, not to make money
and get famous. I wrote it in a rather
dire period of my life. I was not a
screenwriter at that time, I was a
critic and a number of things had
gone wrong in my life. I had ended
up in a period where I was drifting,
living in a car. I had this pain in my
stomach, went to an emergency room
and it turned out I had a bleeding
ulcer. I realised when I was there that
I hadn't really spoken to anyone in
weeks. I'd just been drifting around
and this metaphor of a taxi driver
occurred to me, that I was like this
person in an iron coffin, surrounded
by people, but absolutely alone and
in so many ways I wrote that script so
that I would not become that character.

MARK COUSINS: You said, "It leapt
out of you like an animal..."

PS: Yeah, I mean it had to be written,
and I therefore got involved in
films for the best reasons possible,
which you see less and less today.
I got involved because I needed to
get involved.

MC: You think Taxi Driver has an
ameliorating influence on people.
Do you mean that people who are
potentially psychotic can watch it
and...?

PS: They see... Hopefully it will do for
them in some fashion, what it did for
me. That is, to put that kind of self-

absorption, that kind of festering,
masochistic, narcissistic anger in
a context.

MC: I'd like to look at the end of the
picture, which is incredibly close to
how you wrote it, many years before
it was filmed. You say of Travis...
(reads from the screenplay:)

"He forms his bloody hand into a
pistol, raises it to his forehead and
his voice croaking in pain, makes the
sound of a pistol discharging: Pgghew!
Pgghew! Travis' head slumps against
the sofa, live sound ceases. Overhead
slow motion tracking shot surveys
the damage..." (Figs.1-4)

Now you're writing as a director,
you're writing the shots...

PS: That's the only camera direction
in the whole script. I don't believe
that writers should write camera
instructions. I don't write them for
myself, I don't write them for others.
The only exception to that rule is
when you can only express a certain
mood by a camera instruction. The
mood in that case was complete
detachment from the events, the
God's eye floating view and in order
to get the idea of a God's eye floating
view, I had to do an explanation of an
overhead tracking dolly. Otherwise I
would never put camera instructions
in a script... (Figs.7-9)

MC: Here's the ending that is so
anticipated in your screenplay...

[Travis Bickle (Robert De Niro), covered in blood, sits on the sofa. We see him from a policeman's point of view, whose arm is extended and who points a gun.] (Fig.1)

PS: (watching) This is a shot from Hitchcock... It's from Marnie (1964)... I mean I know Scorsese, I know it's a shot from Marnie...

[Bickle puts his finger to his head as if shooting himself.] (Fig.2)

MC: (watching) This is precisely as you wrote it.

PS: Yeah.

MC: Once Scorsese came on board, did you know that he would shoot it as you wrote it?

PS: That's his bailiwick, you know...

[Cut to an overhead shot of the scene. Bernard Herrmann's music rises and falls, the camera tracks left and back.] (Figs.3-4)

This shot... We were actually on location, it was a building that had been condemned, but they actually had to tear out the floor above this in order to lay rail through the ceiling.

MC: When the camera goes high like this, when it's "The God's eye view", to use your own words, we feel he's dead, don't we? And then he's not dead.

PS: Yes, well that was intended to be kind of fooling the audience, which was... there's another way to look at this.

MC: I've got the very end of the film now, because this is very different from how you wrote it...

[Travis has recovered from the shootings and become a tabloid hero. Betsy (Cybill Shepherd) is more interested in him than before, but he doesn't reciprocate.] (Figs.5-6)

...Here he drives off and in your script he doesn't drive off... she says, "Maybe I'll see you again sometime, huh?"

PS: Ah ha, well you have to understand that of course when they shot the film, she said that line... So you're not talking about a writing or directing decision, you're talking about an editorial decision. And editorially, Marty was moving on somewhere else, which was this notion, which I supported, that the film is a loop which begins where it ends and that the last scene of the film is the opening scene. It can be shown indefinitely, nothing has changed, his pathology is still in place...

[Travis Bickle pulls away from the pavement. We view the city lights through the taxi windshield. Bickle catches his own reflection in the rear-view mirror of the taxi.]

PS: Bob called me up once when we were shooting and said, "You know, do you think this character Travis..." because he was wearing my boots and my shirt at the time...

MC: ...Which is a very scary thing I have to say.

PS: (laughing) ...And he said, "Do you think this character would say this?" I said, "Bob, I'm in Los Angeles, I'm working on something else, you're in New York, you're Travis Bickle, if you think he would say it, odds are, he probably would." (Fig.10)

MC: But it's clear that De Niro understood that you were Travis Bickle... Yes?

PS: Yeah, but that was a serendipity. Three young men at similar stages in their lives, coming across the same story, knowing the same story, knowing how to tell it and why to tell it. (Fig.11) You should never discount the fact of luck in motion pictures and art in general. Sometimes you just get lucky...

10

11

1980s

The endings of
<u>American</u> <u>Gigolo</u> (1980) and
<u>Light</u> <u>Sleeper</u> (1991)
Paul Schrader (Director)

p.134

The half-man,
half-woman walk in
<u>All</u> <u>of</u> <u>Me</u> (1984)
Steve Martin (Actor)

p.148

The endings of
American Gigolo (1980) and   p.135
Light Sleeper (1991)
Paul Schrader (Director)

4TH FEBRUARY 1998, A LOFT IN
LOWER MANHATTAN

MARK COUSINS: One of the key
films for you when you were a critic
was Bresson's Pickpocket (1959).

PAUL SCHRADER: Yeah, still is...

PICKPOCKET
[Michel (Martin Lassalle) has finally
been captured by the police for
pickpocketing, and is now in jail.
Jeanne (Marika Green) comes to
visit him. In an unexpected gesture,
Michel kisses her through the bars.]

MICHEL: Oh Jeanne, what a strange
road I had to take to reach you.
(Figs.4-6)

PS: If I have to pick one scene
to represent all cinema, I'd pick
that scene.

MC: Really? Why?

PS: It's the magical intervention
of the spirit into human affairs...

MC: (pointing to the screen where
the scene is replayed) Explain that.
What's happening there to that man?

PS: You're talking about a cold,
cut-off person, who had been denying
his emotional and spiritual life. In
one bold moment, everything breaks
through and he makes physical contact
with his true life, the life of the heart
and the soul.

MC: This film had a considerable
influence on your own career.
(Schrader laughs) I've got two
scenes, which I think were directly
influenced...

PS: Well... Not influenced, they're
copies! (laughs again)

AMERICAN GIGOLO
[Framed for murder, male prostitute
Julian (Richard Gere) is in prison.
He is visited by senator's wife,
Michelle (Lauren Hutton). They sit
on either side of a glass partition in
the prison meeting room...]

JULIAN: Why did you do it?
MICHELLE: I had no choice. I
love you.

[She puts her hand up to the glass,
Julian follows.]

JULIAN: God Michelle, it's taken
me so long to come to you. (Figs.1-2)

(Schrader watches)

LIGHT SLEEPER
[John LeTour (Willem Dafoe) sits
in a prison meeting room, behind
a desk with a partition. Ann (Susan
Sarandon) sits on the other side.]

LETOUR: Did we ever fuck? You
know, make love?
ANN: What? Well there was that
Christmas party. Everybody got
so stoned and...
LETOUR: No.
ANN: You came over and crashed at
my place once and we slept together.

LETOUR: You were naked.
ANN: We tried.
LETOUR: I was thinking about it, I
realised we never really did. It's one
of the things I think about. One of
the things I look forward to, I've been
looking forward...
ANN: Me too.

[They touch hands]

ANN: Strange how things work. (Fig.3)

PS: In the first one, I actually went
like Bresson, used the Mozart and
the same line. The translation is
something like, "What a strange road
I have taken to come to you." And in
the second one, I was sort of toying
around with how to end Light Sleeper
and I said, "We really should end it
the same way Pickpocket does. Why
not? Just do it, end it the same way,
I don't care..."

MC: He says, "I've been looking
forward", but most of your characters
can't look forward, they're busy
trying to cope with the present.

PS: Well, it's that notion that only
when we accept our imprisonment,
can we be free. Only when we accept
our determined fate, the prison house
of the body, as Calvin would say.
When we accept these limitations,
then we can burst free. And so in
Pickpocket, American Gigolo and
Light Sleeper, it is the imprisoned
man who finally gets freed.

1

2

3

4

**On the domestic scenes in
Raging Bull (1980)
and their stylistic debt to
Italianamerican (1974)
Martin Scorsese (Director)**

25TH MARCH 1998, SCORSESE'S
OFFICE, PARK AVENUE, NEW YORK

MARK COUSINS: The domestic
scenes in Raging Bull have a very
real feel...

MARTIN SCORSESE: Yes well,
that's it exactly, all the non-fight
scenes come right out of
Italianamerican (Scorsese's 1974
documentary about his parents.)

[In a scene from Italianamerican,
Scorsese's parents are sitting on the
sofa in their Manhattan apartment.
His mother tells his father to sit
closer. There's very little camera
movement.] (Fig.2)

MS: (watching) This is the first
scene I shot. I told them they could
just warm up, but in effect they took
over... (Figs.3-4) I began to realise
that it's really character... The camera
records them and doesn't intrude...
If you notice the non-fighting scenes
in Raging Bull, there isn't that much
camera movement. It's pretty much
setting the scene and letting the people
work... Letting the people, not the
actors, but the characters work.
They're there and they're placed in
their environment and just let them
be. Medium shot, close-up, sometimes
a three shot just to see the baby at
the table in the breakfast scene, for
example, which I always liked.

MC: And the fixing of the television
scene.

MS: Yes, the fixing of the television
scene, where it starts off a little wider
in medium shots and then ends up
getting a little closer, just a little
closer, not a lot...

[The camera pans left. Boxer Jake La
Motta (Robert De Niro) is fixing the
TV as his brother Joey (Joe Pesci)
sits on a sofa, similar to the one in
Italianamerican.]

LA MOTTA: How's that?
JOEY: That looks like something.

[La Motta stands up.]

JOEY: Get back, I can't see nothing
with your stomach in the way... Now,
what are you giving me those dirty
looks for? (Fig.1)

...Now what I mean by "the camera
changes position" is, well let's imagine
there's a two shot of us right now,
this way let's say (he indicates a two
shot with his fingers) and at a certain
point in our dialogue the camera
moves over to our right a little bit...
Well why at that point?

You see, you learn that... You take
shots apart, it's quite interesting.
Watch Hitchcock's Dial M For Murder
(1954), watch the dialogue scenes
and see him changing the camera
positions at certain points in time
and then go back and say, "Why on
that line of dialogue?" You see, it's a
subliminal implication of some sort,
where he's intensifying the drama...

30TH APRIL 2001, FOUR SEASONS
RESORT, SANTA BARBARA

MARK COUSINS: You worked
twice with one of the most notorious
directors in modern cinema, Michael
Cimino. First of all in <u>Thunderbolt</u>
<u>and</u> <u>Lightfoot</u> (1974), then in
<u>Heaven's</u> <u>Gate</u>.

JEFF BRIDGES: Well it's so funny,
I remember trying to talk Cimino out
of hiring me for <u>Thunderbolt</u>. I find
myself doing that often, especially if
I like the script and I think – I don't
know why you want me to play this
guy. I don't want to screw it up. He
went, "Yeah, yeah." I'm glad he didn't
listen to me.

MC: That sounds as if you're not
confident of your own talents.

JB: That's probably accurate. I'm
attracted to things that challenge me
and also, because of that, they kind
of repulse me at the same time. I feel
I'm not sure if I'm going to pull this
off, because I've never done it before.
That's led my career down its
particular path.

MC: If that's the case, then does that
mean you're often nervous during
filming or before filming?

JB: Yeah.

MC: And what do you do about that?

JB: Eh… well over the years… I've
learned to kind of make friends with
my fear. But that doesn't go away.

MC: But one critic said, "Jeff Bridges
is the most naturalistic actor there's
ever been", and yet if you are somewhat
anxious about performing, why does
that anxiety not show?

JB: Well the key word is "act".
You're pretending, you know…

MC: It's hard to hide anxiety.

JB: Yeah. (laughs)

MC: That's why they pay you.

JB: Yeah. That's it, that's it…

MC: <u>Heaven's</u> <u>Gate</u> was made six
years after this film and Cimino had
already had the success of <u>The</u> <u>Deer</u>
<u>Hunter</u> (1978), which was acclaimed
and did very well in the box office.
He'd started living in Beverly Hills
and driving a Rolls Royce. Did he
seem like a different man to you?

JB: Well, not a different man. He had
this wonderful success with <u>The</u> <u>Deer</u>
<u>Hunter</u> and the industry was saying,
"What do you want? Anything you
want, we'll give it to you." And he
said, "Well, I've got an idea. This
is like an epic Western." I remember
when I first read the script how
much I liked it and how I thought
that the arc of this main character
(Kris Kristofferson), it's the birth of
a cynic. It's also about a time in this
country, when these cattle barons
owned all this land and were so
powerful and what happened to these
immigrants that came and found
themselves in the middle of Montana

with these terrible winters surrounded by all these walking hamburgers. They started to eat the cows, the ranchers went crazy and hired all these gunmen from Texas to come and execute them. And it was stamped by the President of the United States.

MC: Your character is a saloon owner and at one point, early in the film, Kristofferson reveals to him the fact that there's a list of 125 immigrants who are going to be killed. Your character says, "They can't kill the whole county", but that's what they intended to do. (Figs.1-4)

JB: When Mike came to me with this film, he had a couple of people that he was considering me for. He said, "There's this one guy" and he described this character that I play and I said, "Gee that reminds me of a relative of mine, John Huston Bridges. He was from Arkansas and he followed the gold rush all the way to Alaska and brought his family along, but got what they called the black dog, a terrible depression." So Mike's eyes lit up and called up the set designer and said, "Change all the names of the signs, it's John Bridges." So I'm actually playing my relative in this film.

Cimino wanted to make it very real and he was going after something really unique. I think his intention was to make the actors feel like they had all the time in the world. I found that maddening sometimes, but at other times we did get that little special spark, you know. It was

also quite dangerous. I remember the attack of all the immigrants on the gunmen at the end. The gunmen are in this little circle and here comes this mass, hundreds of immigrants coming... and there were perhaps five or six stuntmen in the whole group and the rest were all hired locals, just dressed up like cowboys. And they've all got full loads, not real bullets but they're full loads, there's Fuller's Earth which is this very fine dust that the camera could see through better than the naked eye, so you have to have more dust than you would think you'd need. So you can't see anything. And here's the group of mercenaries that have been hired, here come the immigrants, and there's two circles formed. One goes this way and another goes like this in circles. They were doing it at top speed and I remember every time we re-cocked the scene, I'd be there on my horse and I'd say, "God, get us through this..." and we'd go off and we'd do that for weeks. The odds are something is going to happen. We had some tough accidents, but we got off all right in it (Figs.5-6).

MC: And I've got here the roller skating sequence...

JB: Oh, that was fun...

[The setting is a large tent called Heaven's Gate. Hundreds of immigrants – Germans, Ukrainians, Russians, Yugoslavs and Irish – have gathered to drink, unwind and skate in a large circle, in formations and on their own. A group of musicians begin to play upbeat folk music.]

JB: (watching) Oh my gosh. Look at this. That guy David Mansfield. He looks like a little kid there. He did the score for the movie. (Figs.8-9)

[John H. Bridges (Bridges) and prostitute Ella "Cattle Kate" Watson (Isabelle Huppert) join a long line of riotous dancers... (Figs.7, 10-12)]

MC: Are you supposed to be drunk in this sequence...?

JB: Yes I am. Oh this is wonderful. This is wonderful. My God, Vilmos Zsigmond who shot it. Wonderful capturing of those times... We all had to learn how to roller skate. So every day if you weren't working you would go to what we fondly called Camp Cimino and you would rehearse and practise all the things you had to do in the movie. I had to go to a cockfighting class. I had to learn Yugoslav and how to roller skate. They really had these kind of things in those days. Guys would come in from punching cattle and they'd just scrape the shit off their shoes, put on their skates, get drunk and go on the town. Can you imagine? Wow.

[Marshal James Averill (Kristofferson) joins the skaters. (Fig.11) The camera tracks round the dancers, the background blurs. The colours, which at the start of the sequence were restricted to browns, golds and pale yellows, are now almost entirely sepia. The music continues. The drunken atmosphere swells.]

Kris Kristofferson and all the members of his band were playing here, so we had great jam sessions after work and when you had some time off. All the guys who weren't acting were just jamming all the time.

For scenes like this, we'd all be assembled in costumes and the feeling was, well we'll show up, we'll do as many takes as we feel like. If we like it, great, if we don't, no pressure. We'll just come back again. So there was no urgency. As an actor, it was frustrating not to know when a performance counts. Because we'd sometimes do forty or sixty takes and we'd never know why we were going on. But we were always looking for that little magic thing to happen. It was kind of maddening sometimes.

MC: And then there was the reaction to the film.

JB: We got one terrible review in the New York Times, when the movie was first seen. Michael had this date to meet, to show it (at the premiere) and was cutting the film right to the very end. I don't think he even saw it completed before it was shown with all those people in the theatre. And you heard that terrible slow hand clap.

MC: When you were watching, before the slow hand claps, did you have a sense that people were hating it?

JB: Yes, because Michael was going after something new, a different cutting rhythm. America at that time was used to that very fast paced cutting. He was going for a much more leisurely thing, so even I, when I first saw it and I was a champion of the film, kept wanting it to cut, but it didn't. It just hung and hung. So it had a slow pace. And that's because I was trying to impose my rhythm on to the film rather than to get the film's rhythm. The more times I see it and I know now what I'm going to see, I'm able to relax and go with the rhythm of the film. And I enjoy the film each time I see it more and more. I think people, after they read that review, it said, "Oh this is the worst movie of all time", they thought, "I'm not going to go see it." This film expert thinks that this is a terrible film and you can't help but look at it through that filter.

MC: So people disliked it, maybe because of the pace and these expectations you were talking about. Did it also get a bad reaction because it was a leftist film? It was arguing that immigrants in this country didn't have this great early experience.

JB: Yeah... I don't think that was responsible for the lack of success. Another thing was that Cimino had banned the press from coming to visit the set, which immediately put them against the project. You had this guy, a young director who had this one hit. Now he thinks he's God. So they were ready to shoot him down. And that all added to it.

MC: Perhaps people in those days wanted epic films just to be thrilling and adventurous, but this had philosophical questions to ask...

JB: Oh absolutely.

MC: Heaven's Gate was the end of an era in a way. It led to the end of United Artists and it was the end of that certain type of director's movie-making.

JB: It certainly didn't help the Western much. I love Westerns.

MC: But any time afterwards that somebody came with a very personal big project, the studios would say, "Look what happened...

JB: ...Heaven's Gate." And you know there are other movies that cost as much as this and there's so much production value on the screen. I can't remember what the final budget was...

MC: I think it went from $7 million to $42 million.

JB: Yeah. $42 million but, you know...

7TH OCTOBER 1998, A LOFT IN NEW YORK

MARK COUSINS: Let's talk about the gallery sequence in <u>Dressed</u> <u>To</u> <u>Kill</u>. What's it there for?

BRIAN DE PALMA: Well, it's based on an idea I had. I used to go to a lot of art galleries. And I had this visual idea of two people following each other through an art gallery and picking each other up and I wanted to shoot it like a kind of a tango. It's something I sort of experienced myself. Then it took me years to figure out what movie to put it in. But I have a lot of ideas like that. They rattle around in my mind and then I have to find a movie where they fit.

[Colour. CinemaScope image. Dissatisfied wife, Kate Miller (Angie Dickinson) sits alone in a gallery, watching other people walk by. As she admires a particular painting, a mysterious man (Kenny Baker) sits down beside her. Initially Dickinson is startled by the stranger but also sexually attracted to him.] (Fig.1)

BDP: Oh, we have this nice widescreen shot. And they're eyeing each other...

[Kate turns to smile and gaze at the stranger. (Fig.2) He turns to her, then promptly turns back to notes he appears to be making about the paintings. Kate looks away, disappointed.]

He's ignoring her. She can't understand it. She's a little offended that this guy doesn't seem to be interested at all. He's basically brushed her off...

[She removes her gloves and admires the large ring on her wedding finger, in the hope that the man will notice it.] (Figs.3-4)

So she's going to show him she's married. She's not really interested anyway. She takes her glove off. That glove is going to figure as an important element later on. And he couldn't care less...

[Suddenly the man stands up leaving Kate sitting there. Standing up, Kate is unaware that she's dropped her glove. She's about to leave, then hesitates and turns to follow the stranger.] (Fig.5)

BDP: Point of view shot, tracking to a steadicam shot.

MC: Do you understand why this film was so controversial?

BDP: Yes. Because it had a particularly brutal murder of a woman in an elevator (Figs.6-9).

MC: Yes. And also before that woman is so brutally murdered, like <u>Psycho</u>, you've got sequences like this one, which encourage people, women in particular, to identify with all the aspects of the film.

BDP: (ironically) And she's so sinful, here, it's a sinful rendezvous she has... It's very interesting... these movies that were so attacked when they came out. <u>Body</u> <u>Double</u> (1984), which was really attacked when it came out, people come up to me today and say, "What a great movie that was." It's amazing, when the political context in which they were so attacked falls away.

But they look at the movie in moral terms, when what it was, is essentially a kind of very intricate visual exercise. Obviously it played on a certain kind of basic sexual theme, but if a movie's going to last, it's going to have to stand on its own, outside a political context in which it was seemingly conceived.

MC: In Britain it came out at the time of the Yorkshire Ripper serial killer.

BDP: Right.

MC: And that added to the heat around this film. But you're using all the techniques of cinema in a sequence like this, to engage people with this women, before you slash her to bits. Soon she's brutally killed in the elevator.

BDP: Well, I've been asked that question a lot, "Why portray such violence towards women?" If you're making a suspense movie and you put somebody in peril, the woman somehow looks more vulnerable than a man. And I like photographing women more than men.

MC: Why does a woman look more vulnerable than a man?

BDP: Because she's smaller, weaker.

MC: Most of Hitchcock's people in peril are men, like Cary Grant. He obviously thought that those men...

BDP: Well, what about <u>Psycho</u>?

MC: Sure.

BDP: Come on. And... what about <u>Notorious</u> (1946)?

MC: Yeah. Or <u>Suspicion</u> (1941).

BDP: Yeah. There are tons of women in peril.

MC: But more so men. It works for men, too, doesn't it?

BDP: If you like photographing men. Why do certain artists paint nude men or paint nude women? I like to photograph women.

MC: In the past you've compared <u>Dressed</u> <u>To</u> <u>Kill</u> to Buñuel's films. Were you thinking of how he photographed Catherine Deneuve, for example, in <u>Belle</u> <u>de</u> <u>jour</u> (1967)? (Fig.10)

BDP: Yeah, they're beautiful. It's about putting them in situations that can justify you photographing them. I loved watching Angie walk through that museum.

MC: I'd like to wind the clock back for a moment. What age were you when your mother discovered that your father was having an affair and how did that affect you?

BDP: I would say when I was in my teens. But with a lot of that stuff, you're not quite sure if that was actually going on or not. My father ultimately married this woman he was allegedly having this affair with. And he's been married to her longer than he was married to my mother. So, you know, you tend to get very prejudiced information. My father was basically unhappily married and he found another woman and stayed with her for the rest of his life.

MC: And your mother took it bad?

BDP: Oh yeah.

MC: And she attempted to commit suicide, is that right?

BDP: Yes. Yes, she did.

MC: How did you react to that?

BDP: Well, I was very much on her side and felt very badly for her. Consequently all the information I got was from my mother, because my father was cut out of having any kind of contact with us really. Only years later did you get the other side of the story.

MC: What's relevant to your work, is that you tried to observe your father during his affair. I read that you climbed trees and tried to photograph him. Is that true?

BDP: Yes, it is.

MC: And given that there's so much voyeurism in your work, that seems to come from those experiences. Is that overstating?

BDP: Well, I just think cinema is a very voyeuristic form. And the point of view shot like the one there in Dressed to Kill is something that's very particular to cinema. So to me it's like a car chase, it's trying to find out what are the things in cinema you work with. This camera that's watching us as we're talking, we're pretending it's not there.

It's sort of, "Who is that person over there?" But he's watching us and the whole audience is there watching us. If I look at that camera, I'm looking right into the eyes of the people watching. They don't like that. They'd rather have me look at you, where they seem to be observing us and we don't know that they're there. And that's the convention of cinema that's completely unique.

MC: But few film-makers emphasise the voyeurism…

BDP: Well, I think few film-makers emphasise the things that are particularly cinematic, not just the point of view shot, but the elements of pure cinema that are a lost art, as far as I can see. Judging from the things that are being made today.

MC: But again, you seem to have had adolescent experiences which relate to the kind of films you made later on. For example, did you dress up, break into your father's office and try to stalk him at night with a knife? Is that a true story?

BDP: Yes, that is a true story.

MC: These are all traumatically disturbing things which must have intensified your fascination with the point of view shot.

BDP: Well it's the fact that you are observing information, like a little detective. And I put this in one of my movies. Yeah, you're kind of collecting information. But it's a little different than observing the kind of an emotional situation in your family and suddenly say, "Ah, this is where the peeping Tom, the sort of voyeuristic aspect of the cinema that interested him comes from." I think the sort of observer over there, the camera, is something that perhaps I was a little more aware of, because I had done it in my life. But it is an element of cinema that is one of the most important ones. And also the close-up, which is particularly cinematic. This big shot that you take, which you can only see in cinema and not in any other artistic form. You can really look into the eyes and the emotions of the actors as they're feeling things.

Overleaf: Brian De Palma behind the camera during the filming of Obsession (1976).

1

2

3

4

The half-man,
half-woman walk in
All of Me (1984)
Steve Martin (Actor)

p.149

26TH NOVEMBER 1997,
FORMOSA CAFE, LOS ANGELES

STEVE MARTIN: ...It had a great script by Phil Robinson, who wrote and directed Field of Dreams (1989). Very interesting guy.

MARK COUSINS: All of Me is a great idea for a movie, a very Steve Martin idea, about the comic conflicts between men and women.

SM: Yeah. Well, it came from a book (Me Two by Ed Davis). And the producer Steve Friedman bought the book and gave it to Phil.

MC: What's the story?

SM: It's about a man who has Lily Tomlin enter half his body and he has to deal with getting her out through the entire movie.

[Roger Cobb (Martin) walks towards the men's room. The right half of his body moves in a feminine way, caused by the presence of the female half of Martin, Edwina (Tomlin). He stops at the door.]

EDWINA: I can't go in there. That's the men's room.
COBB: (yelling) Just shut up and do as I say.

[A passer-by looks on, bemused. Cobb continues in and goes to a urinal above which is a mirror reflecting Edwina looking at him.] (Fig.1)

EDWINA: Don't you ever, ever yell at me again.
COBB: I'm sorry, but this is not my idea of a good time.
EDWINA: I'm not exactly having one of my best days either. I died five minutes ago.

(Martin laughs)

[Close-up of Martin trying and failing to take down his zip.]

COBB: You'll have to do it.
EDWINA: I'll have to do what?
COBB: You know, take it out.
EDWINA: Take what out?
COBB: The little fireman.
EDWINA: The little fireman?
COBB: You know, my penis!
EDWINA: How dare you say penis to a dead person.

MC: And the man and woman walk took quite a bit of rehearsal? (Figs.2-4)

SM: Yes. What we'd do is we'd get me in a room and Lily and Carl (Reiner, director). And Lily would walk across the room as her character and then I would walk across the room fully as her character, and then I'd just try to lose half of her, rather than acquire half of her.

MC: Did you try to be a particularly visual comedian?

SM: When I was doing stand-up I was very, very visual and that's what I always admired in old movies. Within visual comedy you have Jerry Lewis on the one hand, who is only visual, and you have Laurel and Hardy on the other hand who are quite poignant and moving, as well as visual. So that's the struggle between these two things and you don't want to see Jerry Lewis being poignant, so you have to be careful.

1

2

0

3

4

2ND NOVEMBER 1999, AQUARIUM, LONDON ZOO

MARK COUSINS: Okay, I've got here an opening from a film you made in 1986, when you turned forty. By this stage you had two children and you'd had two divorces. It's set in a small town. It's Blue Velvet.

[The camera pans down from the sunny blue sky to a white picket fence beside a bed of red roses.] (Fig.1)

MC: The camera is pointing up...

DAVID LYNCH: It's falling down from the blue sky...

[Cut to a suburban street. A fire engine approaches with a fireman and a Dalmatian standing on it. As it slowly passes by the camera, the fireman waves.] (Fig.2)

MC: Why is he waving so slowly? Is this shot in slow motion?

DL: I believe it is, yes. Not that slow, but probably forty-eight frames or something.

[Cut to a crossing guard beckoning children to cross the road.]

...and that is a little slower too.

MC: Why slow things?

DL: It's a mood. Sometimes you slow things down for a feeling and those things are for abstract reasons. You go so much in film by feeling...

[Cut to a man in his garden as he waters his lawn. The hose gets caught in a bush and the water starts to build up, almost to bursting point. As the man gets annoyed, he suddenly grasps at his throat and collapses. The camera cuts to a mid-shot of the man in spasms with a toddler to the left of the shot and a dog attacking the hose on the right. This occurs in slow motion.] (Figs.3-4)

MC: But it's not obviously a comic feeling you are after is it, it's a dreamy feeling...

DL: Yeah it's more of a... dreamy feeling and it could slide either way and the next things that follow... explain what it is.

[The camera starts to track through the grass in the lawn. The roar on the soundtrack grows. Finally a knot of crawling insects is revealed.]

MC: Do you remember this book (shows him a children's book, Good Times on Our Street)?

DL: I sure do, I haven't seen that for... about... one hundred years!

MC: You've said that some of the images in this book influenced Blue Velvet and sure enough, if you open this book, you've got picket fences and suburban life.

DL: ...there you go man...

MC: So I guess these kind of intense images were lodged in your brain a long time ago...

DL: You don't know where things come from, they can come from memories or they can be triggered. If they are in the memory, stored away... One day, for some reason, they are released and it seems like a brand new idea or an idea comes in from the ether. As it pops, it may be coloured from something that you know, the picture that forms... sometimes reading a book, the pictures that you put together from the past or your imagination kicks.

MC: So say you are sitting somewhere and these ideas are beginning to pop... describe what is happening. Are you closing your eyes, are you seeing pictures or are you scribbling down ideas...?

DL: Well it depends. If they are coming from the ether, they explode maybe with a little bit of electricity and the whole thing is known. In an instant, a certain sized idea can be known immediately. If it is a series, you see the series. And then it is over and the first impression comes with a lot of power, so you remember that is your guide from then on... if you are reading a book, the words start forming pictures and sounds and you are in a movie in the mind. It is coming in and those now are the impressions that you should remember and carry with you as a guide. Then finally it's a whole story and the impressions and you go.

MC: The main character in <u>Blue Velvet</u>, Jeffrey Beaumont, is dressed as you are dressed now, with your shirt done up and apparently he wore the same wristwatch as you.

DL: I have… I don't like wind on my collarbone and that is how that all started… yeah.

MC: And you used to wear three ties?

DL: And that is a sign of… a person who is very insecure and needs protection. I would have worn several coats if I… wasn't so warm where I was… I just felt vulnerable.

MC: Can I point out that ties aren't the best form of protection?

DL: Well they feel good!

MC: And why were you vulnerable?

DL: I was… I don't know why I was… I had things that I wanted to do, but I didn't like being in the world so much. I liked being inside.

MC: Is that agoraphobia?

DL: I have a hair of that.

MC: How has that come about?

DL: It comes about… well, I'm not sure how it comes about, but there are many things to deal with outside the house. Bad things can happen and why bother with that, why not stay inside and do your work?

MC: Yes indeed. Jeffrey Beaumont, he was quite a naive man, he hadn't experienced very much. Is it odd that somebody who had by that stage experienced quite a lot in his life, would project so much of himself onto this almost teenager.

DL: I don't see him as me. I see him as Jeffrey Beaumont and there is some similarity, but it's the idea of just a bit of innocence which is going to experience some things. That happens all through life. Anyway we go along for a while and then certain things happen and it adds more experience. It's experience from the beginning to the end.

MC: You are, I think, around fifty-three now, what age do you feel?

DL: Inside, we are ageless and when we talk to ourselves, it's the same age of person we were talking to when we were little. It's the body that is changing around that ageless centre.

MC: Surely that is not true? I used to be scared of things as a kid and I am not scared of them now. I didn't understand what France was, and I understand it now.

DL: That is not the self that you are talking to, that is the amount of information you have and experience. Knowledge and experience is part of the process. When you mistake a rope for a snake, as soon as you turn the light on you say, "Oh my goodness, that was a rope, and not a snake." But before the light went on, you are

not so sure, but "the self you talk to", that I was talking about is the one that is sort of ageless. Doesn't mean ignorant, it just means… it just doesn't have an age.

MC: Tell me about the making of this scene:

[Nightclub singer, Dorothy Vallens (Isabella Rossellini) kisses the naked Jeffrey (Kyle MacLachlan) after catching the young stranger spying on her from her cupboard. There is a knock at the door. Holding her knife, she orders Jeffrey back into the cupboard. He spies out from the cupboard slats. Dorothy opens the main door. Jeffrey cannot see what's happening. She then backs into view, followed by an agitated and annoyed Frank Booth (Dennis Hopper).] (Figs.5-7)

<u>DOROTHY</u>: <u>Hello</u> <u>baby</u>.
<u>BOOTH</u>: <u>Shut</u> <u>up!</u> <u>It's</u> <u>Daddy</u> <u>you</u> <u>shit</u> <u>head!</u> <u>Where's</u> <u>my</u> <u>bourbon.</u>

MC: Is it true you used a new type of lens here to show as much of the apartment as possible?

DL: No…!

MC: Your cinematographer (Frederick Elmes) said you did!

DL: No… they might have done… that didn't look too wide a lens really.

MC: As a young guy, you had this fantasy of hiding in a girl's room and watching her…

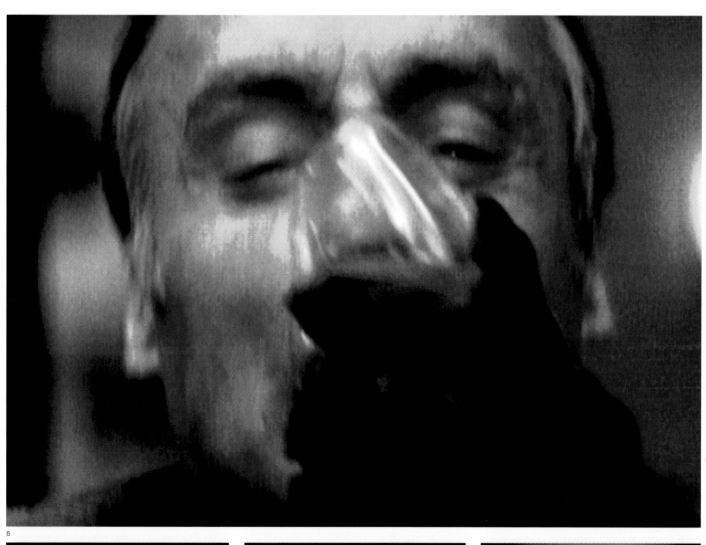

5

6

7

8

DL: Yeah, that is a fantasy... that goes together with many, many other things and a story comes out so... But I remember from that... well it's the opening or just after the opening of another world for Jeffrey. It's Dennis Hopper's first scene... If ever there was anyone born to play the role of Alvin Straight, it was Richard Farnsworth (in Lynch's <u>The Straight Story</u>, 1999) and... the same goes for Dennis Hopper and Frank Booth.

MC: At the end of <u>Blue Velvet</u>, is Jeffrey different from how he was at the start?

DL: For sure, the same but with more knowledge and experience.

MC: He begins to understand that life has an underbelly. And he shoots Frank, but he stays in the small town and goes back to college?

DL: Well we don't know, that is the thing about the film, it starts and then it ends. Nothing should be added and nothing should be taken away and so it's wrong for me to say. But it's beautiful, for anyone to have the right to go where they want to go.

MC: In private, when you are not talking to an interviewer like me or when you are not on television, do you talk more about your films? To your family here?

DL: No... no... they will back me up...

MC: (to Lynch's wife, Mary Sweeney and son, off camera) Do you find it frustrating that he doesn't, or are you happy with that situation?

MARY SWEENEY: Yeah... as long as he keeps making movies!

MC: You once used this phrase, "The eye of the duck scene". What does that mean?

DL: Well, nature can teach us a lot of things and there's something about... in painting, you're working within a certain shaped canvas and there are many things that one does instinctively, to move the eye. There's repetition of shape, colour. But when you look at a duck, you see your eye is moving in a certain way. You see textures, colours and shapes and you start wondering about a duck, what it can teach us about, you know, any kind of abstract painting or proportions or even sequences and scenes. It is always interesting that the eye is in the perfect place. If you move it to the body, it would get lost. If you move it to the leg or the beak, it's two fast areas competing, even though the eye is the fastest, it's the little jewel...

MC: Fast, meaning what?

DL: Well there's slow and fast. An empty room is a certain speed and a person standing there is another speed. That proportion can be beautiful, if the room is a two and the person is a seven. Fire and electricity can go up to a nine, for instance, or a really intricate, decorated room is pretty disturbing sometimes, it's too fast. But then if you put something slow in it, it would work beautifully. A busy room and a person, they fight each other, so...

MC: Is this to do with how fast our eye moves to scan it?

DL: It's a relationship thing, I think. Fast and slow areas.

MC: Okay. What's the eye of the duck scene in <u>The Straight Story</u>?

DL: I haven't thought about it. I have to think about it, I can't just jump in and think... but I believe every film has the eye of the duck scene. But it can fool you, which one it is. It could be the scene we were talking about, I don't know.

MC: What's the eye of the duck scene in <u>Blue Velvet</u>?

DL: I used to know (laughs).

MC: Is it the song, "In Dreams" (by Roy Orbison)?

DL: It's the eye of the duck scene, that's the eye of the duck, yes. Yes.

MC: And what's the eye of the duck scene in <u>The Elephant Man</u> (1980)?

DL: I used to know (laughs).

MC: Is it the scene when he goes to the theatre, near the end?

DL: No, I think strangely the eye of the duck scene is the ending.

MC: Okay. Today, lots of film-makers are using computer-generated imagery and you haven't used that so much. There's still a magic lantern quality about your films, even in <u>Lost</u> <u>Highway</u> (1997), in that transformation from one guy to the other guy, you didn't use a computer to do that. It was all in-camera stuff and it reminds me of the sort of things Jean Cocteau (for example <u>Le</u> <u>sang</u> <u>d'un</u> <u>poète</u>, 1930) was doing. (Fig.8) Why does that appeal to you?

DL: It's organic, and I'm not against computer, you know, the computer or digital or... and I love manipulating images, but film still has the beautiful organic quality. A lot of times with light, emulsion, the way that it's developed and some happy accidents you get something that's thrilling to the soul. I think right now, digital is, coming up every year, but it hasn't matched the beauty of film.

MC: When you're making a much more complex story, for example, in the end of <u>Twin</u> <u>Peaks:</u> <u>Fire</u> <u>Walk</u> <u>With</u> <u>Me</u> (1992), after Laura is killed and we go into the Red Room, a lot of complicated things are happening and still you're using techniques like the Surrealists.

DL: It's the same thing, plus there might have been some way to work by moving over to digital and then coming back to film, but it would have been way too expensive for us.

MC: Except for the screen ratio, that kind of film-making could have been done in the 1920s. And why do you smile when I say that, is that...?

DL: Because, it's beautiful to discover ways of doing things and it's a beautiful medium because it allows so many things to happen.

MC: I remember when I first saw <u>Fire</u> <u>Walk</u> <u>With</u> <u>Me</u> at the Cannes Film Festival, there were loud boos. How does the apparent failure of a film like this affect you?

DL: <u>Dune</u> (1984) was a failure to me because I didn't feel I did the <u>Dune</u> I should have done. This was not a failure to me because I felt it was a film that I did the way I should have done it. So we learn that we can't control anything that happens after a film is finished. Sometimes things go well in the world and sometimes they don't. But if you believe in the film and you've done your best, they can't take that away from you. There's this thing, there's the doughnut, and there's the hole and we should keep our eye on the doughnut and not on the hole.

1990s

The ending of
<u>Goodfellas</u> (1990)
Martin Scorsese (Director)

p.158

The Omaha Beach scenes in
<u>Saving</u> <u>Private</u> <u>Ryan</u> (1998)
Tom Hanks (Actor)

p.176

The "One generation away from
poor white trash" scene in
The Silence of the Lambs (1991)
Jonathan Demme (Director)

p.162

The roots of fear and
discovering Bob in
Twin Peaks: Fire Walk
with Me (1992)
David Lynch (Director)

p.168

The dance routine in
The Adventures of Priscilla
Queen of the Desert (1994)
Terence Stamp (Actor)

p.172

1

2

3

4

5

6

25TH MARCH 1998, SCORSESE'S
OFFICE, PARK AVENUE, NEW YORK

MARK COUSINS: One of your best
films from the 1990s was Goodfellas.
Its style is completely different from
your other films. It's twice as fast as
New York, New York (1977). Why is
it so fast and where did you get the
new style from?

MARTIN SCORSESE: The new style
merely comes from a pure state of
excitement of how I first heard the
famous storytellers. In the old world,
storytellers would move from village
to village. Well, a lot of the guys
who would stand around the street
corners, where I was from, were also
excellent storytellers, funny and self-
deprecating. They'd conjure up images
so quickly. And they were tough kids,
very tough people.

I always said, "Imagine making
a film with that kind of speed and
excitement and humour!" It's what
makes the way of life in this film, at
first, seem extremely romantic and
appealing. But then of course, one
starts to pay for it and you begin to
see what the lifestyle is really about,
just a dead end, a moral, spiritual
dead end. And in some cases just
dead. Some people are killed or put
in jail. It's a joke. Life expectancy is
early twenties or late twenties.

But in any event, I'm a little annoyed
by what was happening in American
films, by things going faster. So I
thought, if you're wanting it fast, I'll
give it fast. Let's go real fast on this

one, because that's the lifestyle, it's
fast! And it's true. You get stopped
by a bullet, a bat on the head or a
cop putting you in and out of jail.
(Figs.5-6)

MC: I have here the ending of the
picture, when he (Henry Hill) has
ratted on his colleagues and now
he has to go and live in isolation
in suburbia. What is the tone of
this ending?

MS: The tone is like he has the
nerve to be complaining. And you're
watching this! What do you feel about
it? I remember Paul Schrader said
to me, "You know Marty, you should
think about that ending, because
people don't want to be sitting for two
hours and twenty minutes for a guy
who reacts that way at the end of the
film." And I said, "But that was kinda
the people I knew growing up, I just
want to deal with it realistically." We
dare the audience to get annoyed. It's
like a provocation.

MC: And he's sent into a mundane
world, instead of an exciting but
scary one.

MS: Yeah, exactly. I'm not saying
people should live this way, but I
want them to understand the thinking,
and if the thinking provokes you to
anger, well then, that's life.

[Henry Hill (Ray Liotta) has testified
in court against his former associates.
In a final monologue he speaks
directly to the camera.]

HENRY: Didn't mean anything. When I was broke I would go out and rob some more.

MS: (watching) See? And everything worked out.

HENRY: We ran everything, paid off cops, paid off lawyers, paid off judges.

MS: The judges particularly, "You don't tell me where to go because I know what you paid for that seat." (Fig.4)

HENRY: Everybody had their hands out. And now it's all over. (Figs.1-2)

MC: Terrible sense of regret.

MS: I know but it's ironic. I mean a regret for what?

[Cut from Henry in the courtroom addressing the camera to a tracking shot along a partially built suburban street.]

HENRY (VOICE-OVER): Today is different. There's no action. I have to wait around like everyone else.

MC: For a good life?

MS: His idea of a good life, which is what we had seen for two hours.

[The camera stops at one house and Henry comes out of the door in a dressing gown. He picks up his newspaper.] (Fig.3)

HENRY (VOICE-OVER): Can't even get decent food. Right after I got here, I ordered spaghetti with marinara sauce and what I got was egg noodles with ketchup.

MS: It's madness. He's complaining about marinara sauce!

HENRY (VOICE-OVER): An average nobody. I get to live the rest of my life like a schmuck.

[Hold on Henry's face as he faintly smiles. Hard cut to the deceased Tommy DeVito (Joe Pesci) shooting a gun into the camera.] (Fig.7)

MC: And why that? This character is already dead in the picture.

MS: That's a reference to The Great Train Robbery (1903), directed by Edwin S. Porter, that's the way that film ends. And the plot of this picture is very similar to The Great Train Robbery. (Fig.8) It hasn't changed in ninety years, it's the same story. The gunshots will always be there. He'll have to watch behind his back, have eyes at the back of his head as they say.

7

8

sequence we wanted huge close-ups of these two every time they're together, (Figs.4-5) because after all, as Scott Glenn says, "Don't let Dr Lecter inside your head." And we went right to the verge of inside his head. Finally, in the scene when he gets her to talk about her past experiences, it's so tight that you can't even see her eyebrows. It's framed right on the bottom of her lower lip which is as close to going inside her head, as we could go. And we used these critical focus long lenses, because if you did a hard (wider angle) lens it wouldn't look as good. The lighting wouldn't be as nice and the features wouldn't be as terrific. It would stretch things out if you moved in that close. (Figs.2-3)

MC: Lecter says there, "Your good bag and your cheap shoes." He's an intellectual snob, isn't he, which is interesting in your work, because you never patronise your working class characters which is quite rare. Here, is there a danger that the fascination of Lecter means that we identify with him too much, even though he's a snob, even though he's a dangerous and violent man?

JD: There was discussion about that at various stages of the process, even when we were preparing. It was, "Gosh this villain is awfully attractive and doesn't this glamorise what he is?" The whole idea of Dr Lecter as portrayed in the book and as performed by Anthony Hopkins is powerful. I look at that face there (pointing to screen) and I see the greatest brain around, but

also tremendous humanity, like Hopkins' character in The Elephant Man, where he was the kindest, deepest doctor. So one of the many things that appealed to me about Tony in the part was this humanity, gone so hideously awry.

In the end, if anyone says, "Didn't you make this mutilating serial killer too attractive?" I would just have to say to them, "Why do you find him so attractive? I think he's appalling."

MC: Humanity you say, yet Hopkins claims that he copied Lecter's tone of voice from Hal in 2001: A Space Odyssey (1968), directed by Stanley Kubrick, which is a computer. It's a machine.

JD: Yes, it's a machine with a voice designed to be tremendously soothing and reassuring. That was the point of Hal's voice.

[The clip resumes.]

LECTER: That accent, you tried so desperately to shed – pure West Virginia. (mimics a Virginian accent) What was your father dear? A coal miner? Did he stink of the lamp? And all those tedious sticky fumblings in the back seats of cars, while you could only think of getting out.

[Clarice listens, her face trying not to register the insults.]

JD: (watching) This illustrates that great acting is listening. It's easy to give a great speech. It's another thing to really listen.

MC: And her eyes are still off centre here, and then, all of a sudden, you and Tak bring the camera round...

LECTER: Getting anywhere, yes? Getting all the way to the F...B...I!

JD: Yeah, because you've got to work yourself into the subjective camera. You can't just pop into it.

STARLING: You see a lot, Doctor. But are you strong enough to point that high-powered perception at yourself? What about it? Why don't you look at yourself and write down what you see? Or maybe you're afraid to.

[Lecter slams the tray containing the information on the Buffalo Bill killings. The clang jolts Starling.]

LECTER: A census taker once tried to test me. I ate his liver with some fava beans and a nice Chianti.

[Lecter hisses and savours.]

MC: Hopkins says that he got that from the movie Bram Stoker's Dracula (1992), directed by Francis Ford Coppola, but I looked and it's not in it.

JD: The sucking noise? I have to say, and I've mentioned this to Tony, it's highly un-Dr Lecter. Although he made it so.

Overleaf: Jonathan Demme directs Jodie Foster in The Silence of the Lambs (1991).

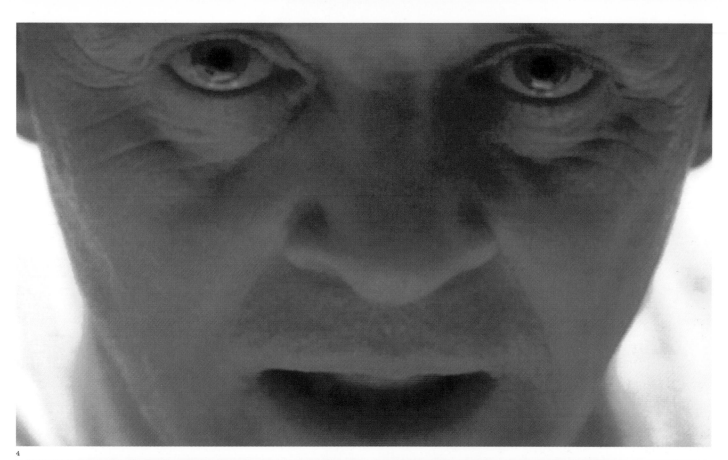

4

5

**The roots of fear and
discovering Bob in
<u>Twin</u> <u>Peaks</u>: <u>Fire</u> <u>Walk</u> <u>with</u> <u>Me</u>
(1992)
David Lynch (Director)**

p.169

2ND NOVEMBER 1999, AQUARIUM, LONDON ZOO

MARK COUSINS: <u>The</u> <u>Elephant</u> <u>Man</u>, it's one of your very few films set in a city isn't it?

DAVID LYNCH: I believe so...

MC: And by the time you made it, you had moved from your childhood small-town and gone to live in Philadelphia which you said, "Was one of the most important influences in your life." It filled you with, as you put it, "An ocean of fear...?"

DL: Wow... Philadelphia was a city filled with fear, filled with twisted behaviour. It is called The City of Brotherly Love. The absence of love was alive and well; there was a sort of a sickness in the air and more of a twisted infectious sickness and a decaying... but it was at the same time, very powerful and a lot of Philadelphia seeped into me. It is a time in life when the window is wide open, things hit you particularly hard and it was a beautiful experience for me.

MC: That seems paradoxical to say... that... this terrifying place was a beautiful experience.

DL: Well it fed many things that came along later.

MC: There seems to be more fear in your films than many others of your generation. There are certainly more monsters like Bob and Frank.

DL: Well, I think there is a mixture of things always in life. In order to have one, you have to have the other. In order to appreciate ups you have to have the downs. Films are made up of contrasts and things that you can't really put your finger on, that are felt more than seen. There are feelings in the air and sometimes those can take on a... persona.

MC: What do you remember of this scene from <u>Twin</u> <u>Peaks</u>: <u>Fire</u> <u>Walk</u> <u>with</u> <u>Me?</u>

[Laura Palmer (Sheryl Lee) walks towards a bedroom door. It opens slowly and gradually reveals the room. A drum beats slowly. As a chest of drawers is revealed in a far corner, a loud scream is heard and there is a fast cut to Laura who has witnessed something terrifying.] (Figs.1-3)

MC: How did you make a scene like this so scary?

DL: Well, that is pretty much common sense... it's the feeling of sensing something, needing to find out but dreading every second.

MC: Is it true that Bob wasn't in the original idea for <u>Twin</u> <u>Peaks</u>?

DL: Right, this is one of the things that can happen and it's a beautiful thing when it does. I was on the set in Laura Palmer's house. We were on the second floor and were going to shoot a panning shot in Laura's room to start with. Frank Silva was the set decorator and he was arranging some furniture. At a certain point, he moved a chest of drawers in front of the door and someone behind me said, "Don't block yourself in there Frank." And... my mind pictured Frank blocked in the room.

[Then we see what Laura has witnessed. Bob (Silva) is hiding behind the dressing table. We see him in close-up. He roars. We see inside his throat. Laura runs out.] (Fig.4)

And then I rushed up to him and said Frank, "Are you an actor?" And he said, "Why, I happen to be an actor" and so I said, "You are going to be in this." So we did a couple of pans without Frank and then I had him kneel down behind the bed and freeze. It panned around and there he was, hard to kind of see right away but if you held for a while, suddenly you just see him. I didn't have a clue what I was going to do with that and then later we were shooting the last setup in the house. It was pretty late at night and it was the scene in which Mrs Palmer (Grace Zabriskie) was smoking a cigarette, distraught on the couch, and playing some scenes in her mind.

[The sequence is exactly as Lynch describes. The scenes she sees are point of view shots of someone at night, walking through vegetation.]

DL: And she sees something mentally and lurches up.

[She lurches up. A glove lifts something. She screams.] (Figs.5-6)

The operator has to crank very fast to catch it, nailed it, perfect. She screams at the top of this thing in a big close-up. I said, "Beautiful" and Sean (Doyle), the operator, said, "No it's not good... not good..." and I said, "What's wrong?" And he says, "Someone was reflected in the mirror" and I said, "Who was reflected in the mirror?" And he said, "Frank was." Then I knew I was onto something! (Figs.7-10)

MC: That was a sign...

DL: A very big sign and it led to many things, that those two events kept unravelling...

MC: That's a real reason for keeping your mind as open as possible isn't it?

DL: Absolutely... a lot of things that happen are... may be food for thought and it can end up being useless, but some of those things are such great gifts you can't imagine.

7

8

9

10

1

2

3

The dance routine in
The <u>Adventures</u> <u>of</u> <u>Priscilla</u>
<u>Queen</u> <u>of</u> <u>the</u> <u>Desert</u> (1994)
Terence Stamp (Actor)

p.173

11TH NOVEMBER 1997, FORTNUM & MASON'S, LONDON

MARK COUSINS: If you had an image in the 90s, it was as a very well-dressed, very dapper, quite sophisticated gentleman. Here's what you did in 1994...

TERENCE STAMP: (not looking towards the screen) I'm going to stay looking at you...

[Bernadette (Stamp), in outrageous turquoise make-up, shocking pink and red feather head-dress with peacock offshoots and a cerise body stocking, lip synchs in close-up.] (Fig.1)

BERNADETTE: (singing) <u>Meeting</u> <u>Mr</u> <u>right,</u> <u>the</u> <u>man</u> <u>of</u> <u>my</u> <u>dreams,</u> <u>the</u> <u>one</u> <u>who</u> <u>showed</u> <u>me</u> <u>true</u> <u>love,</u> <u>or</u> <u>at</u> <u>least</u> <u>that's</u> <u>how</u> <u>it</u> <u>seems...</u>

[Wider shot to reveal a clashing pink basque. Bernadette begins to dance.] (Fig.2)

TS: (laughs)

BERNADETTE: <u>Oh,</u> <u>no,</u> <u>finally</u> <u>it</u> <u>happened</u> <u>to</u> <u>me,</u> <u>right</u> <u>in</u> <u>front</u> <u>of</u> <u>my</u> <u>face,</u> <u>then</u> <u>I</u> <u>just</u> <u>can't</u> <u>deny</u> <u>it.</u>

[Bigger close-up. Bernadette's expression throughout suggests that [s]he'd rather be anywhere than on that stage, in that outfit.]

TS: It was really silly, wasn't it? (Fig.3)

MC: I remember seeing it in Cannes, and someone said, "Ladies and Gentlemen, Miss Terence Stamp", and you walked on. (both laugh)

TS: Oh God, it was a silly movie.

MC: Why did you decide to do a silly movie?

TS: I suppose I was being... well, what you just said. I was thought of as this chilling English villain or this androgynous saintly figure and I just wanted to have fun. But at the end of the day, it's a film, it's visual, so there are practicalities. I had a full body wax and I got high-heeled shoes made, I put false nails on, all that kind of stuff.

MC: And is it true that you copied some of Princess Diana's mannerisms?

TS: Well I didn't really copy, because I don't work like that, but in one particular scene, my ear really started to hurt. As I went to take my earring off, I had a kind of flash of her doing that. But these things just happen in that splash of energy when the film is actually running. (Figs.4-5)

MC: You wanted to look as beautiful as possible in the film, is that right? And they were secretly lighting you from the side and making you look as ugly as possible?

TS: Well, I didn't really want to look as beautiful... I just imagined that because the character was very sympathetic and it was a hymn to

1

2

3

4

5

6

7

8

9TH JANUARY 2001, THE
DORCHESTER HOTEL, LONDON

MARK COUSINS: I've got here a
scene from the opening sequence
of <u>Saving Private Ryan</u>. You and
your men are landing on the beach
at Omaha.

[Captain John Miller (Hanks) and
his patrol approach Omaha Beach
on the 6th June 1944. The sea is
rough. As they disembark the landing
craft, a hail of German bullets sprays
them, tearing flesh, pinging on
metal, whizzing into the sea. It is
the start of one of the most violent
and devastating battles in the Second
World War. The men land on the
beach. Mines explode, soldiers are
slain. Miller emerges from a blood-
stained sea.] (Fig.1)

TOM HANKS: You see the red
water...?

[As Miller collapses, the images move
into slow motion. The soundtrack
grinds down into near silence. Miller's
eyes take in the horrific sight before
him. A young, unarmed soldier
attempts to shelter himself from
the bullets. Flames engulf a group
of men. A mine explodes. Miller's
face is showered with their blood.]

TH: ...We shot this very early on,
probably on the third or fourth day...

[One man, eerily calm, searches for
his arm which has been torn from his
body...] (Figs.2-4)

[Miller turns to his left. He sees
burning men run from their boat,
now an inferno. They scramble for
their lives. Miller puts his helmet on
his head; blood runs down his face.
He runs onto the beach to meet with
his patrol.] (Figs.5-9)

The other fellows had yet to work
because in the story we didn't meet
up with them until we got to the base
of the cliffs. After this day of shooting
and particularly after this sequence
which was done in only two takes,
we had a meal break or something
like that. During that break, I went
and found Eddie Burns (Richard
Reiben), Vin Diesel (Adrian Caparzo)
and a few of the others and I said,
"Guys you'd better hold on to your
hats, because Steven (Spielberg) is
doing something down there that's
unlike anything I've ever been a part
of." The shooting was so visceral. It
was so loud, because of the nature of
the automatic fire. You had 300 guys
firing weapons and the explosions
were quite concussive. You do feel
them even when they're happening
thirty, forty, or even fifty yards away.
On my left, as far down the beach as
I could see, there were men in the
throes of being killed or burned. That
particular image of the soldier looking
for his arm and picking it up is not
exactly what I read in Ambrose's book
(<u>D-Day</u>, by Stephen Ambrose, who
was also a consultant on the film).
But it was so evocative of dozens of
eyewitness accounts, of guys reporting
what they've seen, that you couldn't
help but have the sense that you were
literally in a maelstrom of hell. We

were doing that. And of course we all knew that it was fake. We all knew that we were making a movie, yet what Steven does with the camera creates the sensation of an actual shell shock, of experiencing a round going off near you. And it's a brand of the paralysing fear that John Miller must have been going through. The choice is between getting on with things and seizing up and going nowhere. That's why I had to go up and tell the other actors, "Nothing we've talked about has prepared you for what we're going to do now..."

MC: Presumably Spielberg had said, "Look this is going to be rougher than you can imagine?"

TH: Well you know Steven doesn't necessarily communicate in that way. You just have to get there and see the scope of what he's doing and you immediately get into the spirit of things. It's infectious. That was as big a tableau as I've ever encountered in motion pictures. More people, the physical manifestation of the place, the sea, just the fact that before the cameras rolled the prop guys unbeknownst to me came and threw all that blood in the water. That ends up being a very tactile acting experience, that is not nearly equal to the real thing, but is nonetheless substantially emotional for us to go through, even though we're professional actors.

MC: And do you think it's right for a director, say somebody like Alfred Hitchcock, not to tell the actor everything that's going to happen to them, thereby playing on their real fears and their real sense of surprise?

TH: Well, I think that that is possible to do to some degree, but not if it's actually going to be endangering. All sorts of stuff happens quite by accident, but if a director was going to try to get something out of me without making me privy to what it was and it ends up being dangerous or uncomfortable, I'm going to lose confidence in him, because he doesn't have any confidence in me. I pride myself on my ability to get to a certain place.

MC: Saving Private Ryan is a morally serious film. It tries to honour the generation of our fathers who fought in the Second World War. Do you think that they, in general, had more to deal with in their lives? That their generation was more challenged than ours?

TH: Well, their challenges were more clearly delineated. I think that all of our struggles are quite relative and I don't discount anything that any generation is going through. Teenagers now are facing a brand of challenge that is different, but equal to those faced by this generation. They had gone through the great depression, then they entered early adulthood faced with these two evil empires, Nazis and Soviets, that were trying to take over the world. That's a very clear challenge which required obvious moral choices to be made. Today, moral choices are much more obscure, but equally difficult.

9

1940s

To Have and Have Not (1944)
Prod. Co. Warner Bros.
Exec. Prod. Jack L. Warner
Dir. Howard Hawks
Scrs Jules Furthman,
William Faulkner
Ph. Sid Hickox
Art Dir. Charles Novi
Ed. Christian Nyby
Music Franz Waxman
Cast Lauren Bacall (Marie 'Slim'
Browning), Humphrey Bogart
(Harry 'Steve' Morgan),
Walter Brennan (Eddie),
Marcel Dalio (Gerard), Hoagy
Carmichael (Cricket), Dolores
Moran (Helene de Brusac),
Walter Molnar (Paul de Brusac)

1950s

The Bad and The Beautiful (1952)
Prod. Co. MGM
Prod. John Houseman
Dir. Vincente Minnelli
Scr. Charles Schnee
Ph. Robert Surtees
Art Dirs Cedric Gibbons,
Edward Carfagno
Ed. Conrad A. Nervig
Music David Raksin
Cast Kirk Douglas (Jonathan
Shields), Lana Turner (Georgia
Lorrison), Dick Powell (James
Lee Bartlow), Walter Pidgeon
(Harry Pebbel), Barry Sullivan
(Fred Amiel), Gloria Grahame
(Rosemary Bartlow), Gilbert
Roland (Victor 'Gaucho' Ribera)

Gentlemen Prefer Blondes (1953)
Prod. Co. Twentieth Century-Fox
Prod. Sol C. Siegel
Dir. Howard Hawks
Scr. Charles Lederer
Ph. Harry J. Wild
Art Dirs Lyle Wheeler,
Joseph C. Wright
Ed. Hugh S. Fowler
Music Jule Styne,
Leo Robin, Hoagy Carmichael,
Harold Adamson
Cast Jane Russell (Dorothy Shaw),
Marilyn Monroe (Lorelei Lee),
Jamie Russell (Olympic team
member), Charles Coburn (Sir
Francis Beekman), Elliott Reid
(Ernie Malone), Tommy Noonan
(Gus Esmond), George Winslow
(Henry Spofford III)

On the Waterfront (1954)
Prod. Co. Columbia
Prod. Sam Spiegel
Dir. Elia Kazan
Scr. Budd Schulberg
Ph. Boris Kaufman
Art Dir. Richard Day
Ed. Gene Milford
Music Leonard Bernstein
Cast Rod Steiger (Charley
Malloy), Marlon Brando
(Terry Malloy), Karl Malden
(Father Barry), Lee J. Cobb
(Johnny Friendly), Eva Marie
Saint (Edi Doyle), Pat Henning
('Kayo' Dugan), James
Westerfield (Big Mac)

Rebel Without a Cause (1955)
Prod. Co. Warner Bros.
Prod. David Weisbart
Dir. Nicholas Ray
Scr. Stewart Stern
Ph. Ernest Haller
Art Dir. Malcolm Bert
Ed. William Ziegler
Music Leonard Rosenman
Cast Dennis Hopper (Goon),
James Dean (Jim Stark), Corey
Allen (Buzz Connors), Natalie
Wood (Judy), Sal Mineo (Jon
'Plato' Crawford), Jim Backus
(Frank Stark), Nick Adams (Moose)

The Big Knife (1955)
Prod. Cos Associates/Aldrich
Prod./Dir. Robert Aldrich
Scr. James Poe
Ph. Ernest Laszlo
Art Dir. William Glasgow
Ed. Michael Luciano
Music Frank De Vol
Cast Rod Steiger (Stanley Hoff),
Jack Palance (Charles Castle),
Ida Lupino (Marion Castle),
Wendell Corey (Smiley Coy),
Jean Hagen (Connie Bliss),
Everett Sloane (Nat Danziger),
Shelley Winters (Dixie Evans)

Touch of Evil (1958)
Prod. Co. Universal
Prod. Albert Zugsmith
Dir. Orson Welles
Scrs Orson Welles, Paul Monash
Ph. Russell Metty
Art Dirs Alexander Golitzen,
Robert Clatworthy
Eds Virgil Vogel, Aaron Stell,
Edward Curtiss, Ernest Nims
Music Henry Mancini
Cast Janet Leigh (Susan Vargas),
Charlton Heston (Ramon Miguel
'Mike' Vargas), Dan White
(Customs Officer), Orson Welles
(Hank Quinlan), Joseph Calleia
(Pete Menzies), Akim Tamiroff
('Uncle' Joe Grandi)

Some Like it Hot (1959)
Prod. Co. Mirisch Company
Prod./Dir. Billy Wilder
Scrs Billy Wilder, I.A.L. Diamond
Ph. Charles Lang Jnr
Art Dir. Ted Howarth
Ed. Arthur P. Schmidt
Music Adolph Deutsch
Cast Jack Lemmon
(Jerry/Daphne), Tony Curtis
(Joe/Josephine), Marilyn Monroe
(Sugar Kane), Joe E. Brown
(Osgood Fielding III),
Joan Shawlee (Sweet Sue),
Billy Gray (Sig Poliakoff),
Dave Barry (Beinstock)

1960s

The Magnificent Seven (1960)
Prod. Cos Mirisch/Alpha Company
Prod./Dir. John Sturges
Scrs William Roberts,
Walter Newman
Ph. Charles Lang Jnr
Art Dir. Edward Fitzgerald
Ed. Ferris Webster
Music Elmer Bernstein
Cast James Coburn (Britt),
Bob Wilke (Wallace), Yul Brynner
(Chris Adams), Horst Buchholz
(Chico), Steve McQueen (Vin),
Charles Bronson (Bernardo
O'Reilly), Robert Vaughn (Lee),
Brad Dexter (Harry Luck)

Spartacus (1960)
Prod. Cos Universal/Bryna
Prod. Edward Lewis
Dirs Anthony Mann,
Stanley Kubrick
Scr. Dalton Trumbo
Ph. Russell Metty
Prod. Des. Alexander Golitzen
Ed. Robert Lawrence
Music Alex North
Cast Kirk Douglas (Spartacus),
Laurence Olivier (Marcus
Licinius Crassus), Jean Simmons
(Varinia), Charles Laughton
(Sempronius Gracchus),
Peter Ustinov (Lentulus
Batiatus), Woody Strode (Draba),
Tony Curtis (Antoninus)

Psycho (1960)
Prod. Cos Paramount/Shamley
Prod./Dir. Alfred Hitchcock
Scr. Joseph Stefano
Ph. John L. Russell
Art Dirs Joseph Hurley,
Robert Clatworthy
Ed. George Tomasini
Music Bernard Herrmann
Cast Janet Leigh (Marion Crane),
Anthony Perkins (Norman
Bates), Vera Miles (Lila Crane),
John Gavin (Sam Loomis),
Martin Balsam (Milton
Arbogast), John McIntire
(Sheriff Al Chambers), Simon
Oakland (Dr Richmond)

Dr. No (1962)
Prod. Co. Eon
Prods Harry Saltzman,
Albert R. Broccoli
Dir. Terence Young
Scrs Richard Maibaum, Johanna
Harwood, Berkeley Mather
Ph. Ted Moore
Prod. Des. Ken Adam
Ed. Peter Hunt
Music Monty Norman
Cast Sean Connery (James
Bond), Ursula Andress (Honey
Ryder), Joseph Wiseman (Dr
No), Jack Lord (Felix Leiter),
Tim Moxon (Strangways),
Bernard Lee ('M'), Lois Maxwell
(Miss Moneypenny)

The Manchurian Candidate (1962)
Prod. Co. United Artists
Prods George Axelrod,
John Frankenheimer
Dir. John Frankenheimer
Scr. George Axelrod
Ph. Lionel Lindon
Prod. Des. Richard Sylbert
Ed. Ferris Webster
Music David Amram
Cast Janet Leigh (Eugenie Rose 'Rosie' Cheyney), Frank Sinatra (Bennett Marco), Laurence Harvey (Raymond Shaw), Angela Lansbury (Eleanor Shaw Iselin), Henry Silva (Chunjin), James Gregory (Senator John Yerkes Iselin), Leslie Parrish (Jocie Jordon)

Marnie (1964)
Prod. Cos Universal/Geoffrey Stanley Inc.
Prod./Dir. Alfred Hitchcock
Scr. Jay Presson Allen
Ph. Robert Burks
Prod. Des. Robert Boyle
Ed. George Tomasini
Music Bernard Herrmann
Cast Sean Connery (Mark Rutland), Tippi Hedren (Marnie Edgar), Diane Baker (Lil Mainwaring), Martin Gabel (Sidney Strutt), Louise Latham (Bernice Edgar), Bob Sweeney (Cousin Bob), Alan Napier (Mr Rutland)

Rosemary's Baby (1968)
Prod. Cos Paramount/William Castle Enterprises
Prod. William Castle
Dir. Roman Polanski
Scr. Roman Polanski
Ph. William Fraker
Prod. Des. Richard Sylbert
Eds Sam O'Steen, Bob Wyman
Music Krzysztof Komeda
Cast Mia Farrow (Rosemary Woodhouse), John Cassavetes (Guy Woodhouse), Ruth Gordon (Minnie Castevet), Sidney Blackmer (Roman Castevet), Maurice Evans (Edward 'Hutch' Hutchins), Ralph Bellamy (Dr Abraham Sapirstein), Angela Dorian (Terry Gionoffrio)

Teorema (1968)
Prod. Co. Aetos Film
Prods Franco Rossellini, Manolo Bolognini
Dir. Pier Paolo Pasolini
Scr. Pier Paolo Pasolini
Ph. Giuseppe Ruzzolini
Art Dir. Luciano Puccini
Ed. Nino Baragli
Music Ennio Morricone
Cast Terence Stamp (The Visitor), Silvana Mangano (Lucia), Massimo Girotti (Paolo), Anne Wiazemsky (Odetta), Laura Betti (Emilia), Andres Jose Cruz (Pietro), Ninetto Davoli (Angelino)

Partner (1968)
Prod. Co. Red Film
Prod. Giovanni Bertolucci
Dir. Bernardo Bertolucci
Scr. Ganni Amico
Ph. Ugo Piccone
Art Dir. Francesco Tullio-Altan
Ed. Roberto Perpignani
Music Ennio Morricone
Cast Pierre Clementi (Jacob I/Jacob II), Stefania Sandrelli (Clara), Tina Aumont (Salesgirl), Sergio Tofano (Petrushka), Giulio Cesare Castello (Professor Mozzoni), Romano Costa (Clara's father), Antonio Maestri ('Tre Zampe', Professor of Drama)

Easy Rider (1969)
Prod. Cos Pando Company/Raybert
Prod. Peter Fonda
Dir. Dennis Hopper
Scrs Peter Fonda, Dennis Hopper, Terry Southern
Ph. Laszlo Kovacs
Art Dir. Jerry Kay
Ed. Donn Cambern
Music Hoyt Axton, Mars Bonfire
Cast Dennis Hopper (Billy), Peter Fonda (Wyatt), Jack Nicholson (George Hanson), Luana Anders (Lisa), Toni Basil (Mary), Karen Black (Karen), Sabrina Scharf (Sarah)

1970s

The Last Movie (1971)
Prod. Cos Alta-Light Productions/Universal
Prod. Paul Lewis
Dir. Dennis Hopper
Scr. Stewart Stern
Ph. Laszlo Kovacs
Art Dir. Leon Ericksen
Supervising Ed. Dennis Hopper
Eds David Berlatsky, Antranig Mahakian
Music Kris Kristofferson, John Buck Wilkin, Chabuca Granda, Severn Darden
Cast Dennis Hopper (Kansas), Stella Garcia (Maria), Julie Adams (Mrs Anderson), Tomas Milian (Priest), Samuel Fuller (Director), Don Gordon (Neville Robey), Roy Engel (Harry Anderson)

Macbeth (1971)
Prod. Co. Playboy Productions
Prod. Andrew Braunsberg
Dir. Roman Polanski
Scrs Roman Polanski, Kenneth Tynan
Ph. Gilbert Taylor
Prod. Des. Wilfrid Shingleton
Ed. Alastair MacIntyre
Music Third Ear Band
Cast Diane Fletcher (Lady Macduff), Mark Digham (Macduff's son), Michael Balfour (1st Murderer), Andrew McCulloch (2nd Murderer), Jon Finch (Macbeth), Francesca Annis (Lady Macbeth), Martin Shaw (Banquo), Nicholas Selby (Duncan)

Fat City (1972)
Prod. Cos Rastar/Columbia
Prod. Ray Stark
Dir. John Huston
Scr. Leonard Gardner
Ph. Conrad Hall
Prod. Des. Richard Sylbert
Ed. Margaret Booth
Music Marvin Hamlisch
Cast Jeff Bridges (Ernie Munger), Stacy Keach (Billy Tully), Susan Tyrrell (Oma), Candy Clark (Faye), Nicholas Colasanto (Ruben), Art Aragon (Babe), Curtis Cokes (Earl)

Last Tango in Paris (1972)
Prod. Cos P.E.A./Productions Artistes Associés
Prod. Alberto Grimaldi
Dir. Bernardo Bertolucci
Scrs Bernardo Bertolucci, Franco Arcalli
Ph. Vittorio Storaro
Art Dir. Ferdinando Scarfiotti
Eds. Franco Arcalli in collabortion with Roberto Perpignani
Music Oliver Nelson
Cast Marlon Brando (Paul), Maria Schneider (Jeanne), Maria Michi (Rosa's mother), Giovanni Galletti (prostitute), Gitt Magrini (Jeanne's mother), Catherine Breillat (Mouchette), Jean-Pierre Léaud (Tom)

Don't Look Now (1973)
Prod. Cos D.L.N. Ventures Partnership/Casey/Eldorado
Prod. Peter Katz
Dir. Nicolas Roeg
Scrs Allan Scott, Chris Bryant
Ph. Anthony Richmond
Art Dir. Giovanni Soccol
Ed. Graeme Clifford
Music Pino Donnagio
Cast Donald Sutherland (John Baxter), Julie Christie (Laura Baxter), Sharon Williams (Christine Baxter), Nicholas Salter (Jonny Baxter), Hilary Mason (Heather), Clelia Matania (Wendy), Adelina Poerio (dwarf)

Save the Tiger (1973)
Prod. Co. Paramount
Prod. Steve Shagan
Dir. John G. Avildsen
Scr. Steve Shagan
Ph. James Crabe
Art Dir. Jack T. Collis
Ed. David Bretherton
Music Marvin Hamlisch
Cast Jack Lemmon (Harry Stoner), Jack Gilford (Phil Greene), Laurie Heineman (Myra), Norman Burton (Fred Mirrell), Patricia Smith

Bibliography selected by
Mark Cousins

Introduction

Truffaut, F. (1968) Hitchcock
by Truffaut (Secker and Warburg,
London).
Gombrich, E.H. (1995) The
Story of Art, sixteenth edition
(Phaidon Press, London).

Lauren Bacall

Bacall, L. (1979) By Myself
(Knopf, New York).
Bacall, L. (1994) Now (Century,
London).
Buckley, M. (1992) 'Lauren
Bacall', Films in Review **XLIII**
(5/6) 152-3.
Domarchi, J. (1958) 'The
Cobweb', Cahiers du Cinéma **XV**
(87) 52-4.
Greenberger, H. (1978) Bogey's
Baby (St Martin's Press, New
York).
Halliday, J. (1971) Sirk on Sirk
(Secker and Warburg, London).
Harvey, S. (1989) Directed by
Vincente Minnelli (Museum
of Modern Art/Harper & Row,
New York).
Hyams, J. (1976) Bogart and
Bacall (Warner Bros. Books,
New York).
Interim, L. (1981) 'Written on
the Wind', Cahiers du Cinéma
329 60-1.
Kyrou, A. (1958) 'La Femme
Modèle (Designing Women)',
Positif **27** 43-5.
Parish, J.P. and Stanke, D.E.
(1980) 'Lauren Bacall' in
Forties Gals (Arlington House,
Connecticut).
Quirk, L.J. (1986) The Films
of Lauren Bacall (Citadel Press,
New Jersey).
Shaw, D.G. (1997) 'Individual
Commitment in To Have and
Have Not', Film and History
Journal **27** (1-4) 72-9.

Bernardo Bertolucci

Bachmann, G. (1973) '"Every
Sexual Relationship is
Condemned": An Interview
with Bernardo Bertolucci
Apropos Last Tango in Paris',
Film Quarterly **XXVI** (3) 2-9.
Bertolucci, A. (1993) Selected
Poems (Bloodaxe Books, Tarset).
Bertolucci, B. (1996) 'Guilty
Pleasures', Film Comment **32**
(4) 80-2.
Bonitzer, P. and Daney, S.
(1981) 'Entretien avec Bertolucci,
on Tragedy of a Ridiculous Man',
Cahiers du Cinéma **331** 24-33.
Ciment, M. and Legrand, G.
(1979) 'Entretien avec
Bertolucci, on Tragedy of a
Ridiculous Man', Positif **224**
29-35.
Gow, G. (1978) 'Cinema and
Life', Films and Filming, **24**
(9) 10-15.
Kolker, R.P. (1985)
Bernardo Bertolucci (BFI
Publishing, London).
Loshitzky, Y. (1995)
The Radical Faces of Godard and
Bertolucci (Wayne State University
Press, Michigan).
Nowell-Smith, G. (1998)
'Journey's From Italy', Pix **2**
176-9.
Roud, R. (1979) 'Bertolucci on
La Luna interviewed by Richard
Roud', Sight and Sound **48** (4)
236-9.
**Sklarew, B.H., Kaufman,
B.S., Handler Spitz, E. and
Borden, D.** (eds) (1998)
Bertolucci's The Last Emperor –
Multiple Takes (Wayne State
University Press, Michigan).
Skorecki, L. (1981) 'Un Homme
Comme les Autres' (Tragedy of a
Ridiculous Man), Cahiers du
Cinéma **329** 50-1.
Thompson, D. (1998) Last
Tango In Paris (BFI Modern
Classics, London).
Tonetti, C.M. (1995) Bernardo
Bertolucci (Twayne Publishers,
New York).
Ungari, E. with Ranvaud, D.
(eds) (1987) Bertolucci by

Bertolucci (Plexus, London).
Young, D. (1977) 'History
Lessons: Bernardo Bertolucci
interviewed by Deborah Young',
Film Comment **13** (6) 16-19.

Jeff Bridges

Aghed, J. and Ciment, M.
(1972) 'Deux Soirées avec John
Huston', Positif **142** 93-104.
Andrew, G. (1988) 'Motor
Mouths' (Tucker), Time Out **950**
16-17,19.
Andrew, G. (1988) 'On Jeff
Bridges', Time Out **954** 33.
Andrew, G. (1988) 'Bridges'
Way', National Film Theatre
Programme (December) 4.
Benayoun, R. (1972) 'La part
de l'ombre sur Fat City, de John
Huston', Positif **142** 89-92.
Burns, M. (1998) 'Heaven's
Gate Takes a Swing: Slamming
the Capitalist Patriarchy',
Cineaction **46** 48-55.
Ciment, M. and Henry, M.
(1981) 'Nouvel Entretien avec
Michael Cimino (A Propos de
Heaven's Gate)', Positif **246**
17-21.
Ciment, M. and Niogret, H.
(1998) 'Entretien avec Joel et
Ethan Coen', Positif **447** 8-11.
Combs, R. (1981) Heaven's Gate,
Monthly Film Bulletin **48** (573)
200-1.
Coursodon, J-P. (1981)
'Controverses et Feux Croisés sur
Les Portes Du Ciel', Cinéma (Fr.)
266 4-23.
Eyquem, O. and Thomas, F.
(1989) 'Entretien avec Francis
Ford Coppola', Positif **335** 5-9.
Fennell, T. (1994) 'The Art of
Cool' (Fearless), Empire **59** 70-4.
French, S. (1988/9) 'Retread'
(Tucker), Sight and Sound **58**
(1) 88-9.
Gray, M. (1994) 'The
Fabulous Bridges Boy', Empire
19 48-50, 52.
Kael, P. (1971) 'The Last
Picture Show', Filmfacts **XIV**
(15) 362-3.
Lindroth, J. (1989) 'From
Natty to Cymbeline: Literary

Figures and Allusions in
Cimino's Heaven's Gate',
Literature/Film Quarterly **17**
(4) 224-30.
Milne, T. (1990) 'The Fabulous
Baker Boys', Monthly Film
Bulletin **57** (674) 67-9.
Murray, S. (1994) 'Fearless',
Cinema Papers **100** 67-8.
Pym, J. (1986) 'Almost Anarchy,
Afterthoughts on Heaven's Gate',
Sight and Sound **51** (1) 20-4.
Romney, J. (1998) 'The Big
Lebowski', Sight and Sound **8** (5)
38-9.
Royal, S. (1989) 'The Fabulous
Bridges Boys: An Interview with
Beau and Jeff Bridges', American
Premiere **IX** (5) 14-20.
Smith, S.M. (1998) 'Pin City:
On the set of The Big Lebowski,'
Premiere (USA) **11** (7) 78-83.
Snow, M. (1991) 'Spot the
Difference' (Texasville and The
Last Picture Show), Empire **19**
48-50, 52.
Southgate, M. (1993) 'Fearless,
Flying', Premiere (USA) **7** (2)
50-3.
Stenberg, D. (1994) 'Tom's a-
cold – Common Themes of
Transformation and Redemption
in King Lear and the The Fisher
King', Literature/Film Quarterly
22 (3) 160-9.
Stukator, A. (1997) '"Soft
Males", "Flying Boys", and
"White Knights": New
Masculinity in The Fisher King',
Literature/Film Quarterly **25** (3)
214-221.

James Coburn

Bulnes, J. (1983) 'Le
Philosophe de Hollywood',
Cine Révue **63** (45) 16-19.
Butler, T. (1979) Crucified
Heroes (Gordon Fraser, London).
Gow, G. (1978) 'Becoming
Involved', Films and Filming **25**
(2) 12-16.
Hanson, C.L. (1965) 'James
Coburn on Acting, Directors,
Hollywood and Movies', Cinema
3 (1) 11-13.
Leydon, J. (1975) 'His Life and

Hard Times', Take One **4** (12) 6-8.
Roberts, J. (1995) 'James Coburn and Cross of Iron' in **Roberts, J. and Gaydos, S.** (eds) Movie Talk from the Front Lines: Filmmakers Discuss Their Works with the Los Angeles Film Critics Association (McFarland and Company Inc., Jefferson).
Simmons, G. (1998) Peckinpah: A Portrait in Montage (Limelight Editions, New York).
Weddle, D. (1994) Sam Peckinpah: If They Move... Kill 'Em! (Faber and Faber, London).

Sean Connery

Cousins, M. (1997) 'Kiss Kiss, Bang Bang', The Scotsman **03.05.97** 5-7.
Cousins, M. (1997) 'King of the Hill', Sight and Sound **7** (5) 22-4.
Freedland, M. (1995) Sean Connery: A Biography (Orion, London).
Jackson, K. (1991) 'With a Licence to Thrill', The Independent **16.02.90** 30.
Pfeiffer, L. and Philip, L. (1993) The Films of Sean Connery (Citadel Press, New Jersey).

Jonathan Demme

Andrew, G. (1987) 'Demme Monde', Time Out **880** 20-1.
Bliss, M. and Banks, C. (1996) What Goes Around Comes Around – The Films of Jonathan Demme, (Southern Illinois University Press, Carbondale and Edwardsville).
Clarens, C. (1980) 'Demme Monde, Jonathan Demme interviewed by Carlos Clarens', Film Comment **16** (5) 56-9.
Henry, M. and Niogret, H. (1989) 'Entretien avec Demme', Positif **335** 24-32.
Smith, G. (1991) 'Identity Check, Jonathan Demme interviewed by Gavin Smith', Film Comment **27** (1) 28-30, 33-7.

Sragow, M. (1984) 'Jonathan Demme: On the Line', American Film **IX** (4) 44-7,80.
Taubin, A. (1994) 'The Odd Couple', Sight and Sound **4** (3) 24-5.
Vineberg, S. (1991) 'Swing Shift, a tale of Hollywood', Sight and Sound **60** (1) 8-13.

Brian De Palma

Bliss, M. (1983) Brian De Palma (Scarecrow, Metuchen, New Jersey).
Bouzereau, L. (1996) Ultra Violent Movies (Citadel Press, New Jersey).
Brown, R.S. (1977) 'Considering De Palma', American Film **II** (9) 54-61.
Daney, S. and Rosenbaum, J. (1982) 'Entretien avec Brian De Palma', Cahiers du Cinéma **334-5** 14-8,127.
De Palma, B. (1987) 'Guilty Pleasures', Film Comment **23** (3) 52-3.
Dworkin, S. (1984) Double De Palma (Newmarket Press, New York).
Henry, M. (1977) 'L'oeil du malin à propos de Brian de Palma', Positif **193** 17-22.
Henry, M. (1977) 'Entretien avec Brian De Palma', Positif **193** 23-31.
Keough, P. (1992) 'Out of the Ashes', Sight and Sound **2** (8) 14-15.
MacKinnon, K. (1990) Misogyny in the Movies – The Brian De Palma Question (Associated University Presses, New Jersey).
Mandell, P. (1978) 'Brian De Palma discusses The Fury', Filmmakers Newsletter **11** (7) 26-31.
Rafferty, T. (1984) 'De Palma's American Dreams', Sight and Sound **53** (2) 142-6.
White, A. (1991) 'Brian De Palma, Political Filmmaker', Film Comment, **27** (3) 72-8.

Kirk Douglas

Buckley, M. (1989) 'Kirk Douglas', Films in Review **XL** (8/9) 386-396 and **XL** (10) 458-473.
Ciment, M. and Tavernier, B. (1970) 'Propos de Kirk Douglas', Positif **112** 12-18.
Cooper, D. (1991) 'Who Killed Spartacus', Cineaste **XVIII** (3) 18-27.
Dawson, J. (1996) 'Captain Kirk', Empire **61** 86-93.
Douglas, K. (1988) The Ragman's Son (Simon and Schuster Inc, New York).
Douglas, K. (1997) Climbing the Mountain: My Search for Meaning (Simon & Schuster, New York).
Gow, G. (1972) 'Impact', Films and Filming **18** (12) 216 10-14.
Thomas, T. (1991) The Films of Kirk Douglas (First Carol Publishing, New Jersey).
Thompson, F. (1991) 'Spartacus: A Spectacle Revisited', American Cinematographer **72** (5) 35-40.
Trumbo, D. (1991) 'Large Spartacus and Small Spartacus', Cineaste **XVIII** (3) 30-3.

Tom Hanks

Anderson, K. (1998) 'The Tom Hanks Phenomenon: How Did He Pull it off', New Yorker **07/14.12.98** 104, 106, 115-6, 118-20, 122-4, 127-8.
Barber, L. (1997) 'Hankie Not Hunkie', Observer Life Magazine **19.01.97** 6, 8.
Dawson, J. (1994) 'God Bless America', Empire **65** 100-3, 105, 107, 109, 110-11.
Doherty, T. (1998) 'Saving Private Ryan', Cineaste **XXIV** (1) 68-71.
Green, J. (1994) 'Philadelphia', Premiere (USA) **7** (5) 54-61.
Murray, S. (1998) 'Saving Private Ryan', Cinema Papers, **128** 43-4.
Pfeiffer, L. and Lewis, M. (1996) The Films of Tom Hanks

(Citadel Press, New Jersey).
Taubin, A. (1994) 'The Odd Couple', Sight and Sound **4** (3) 24-5.
Walker, M. (1994) 'Making Saccharine Taste Sour', Sight and Sound **4** (10) 16-17.

Dennis Hopper

Carcassonne, P. (1981) 'Rencontre avec Dennis Hopper', Cinematographe **68** 77.
Combs, R. (1981) 'Out of the Blue', Monthly Film Bulletin **48** (574) 223-4.
Cullum, P. (1997) 'Living in Oblivion', Neon (June) 70-4.
Goodwin, M. (1970) 'Hopper Rides Again', Premiere (USA), **6** 30-3.
Goodwin, R. (1998) 'The Rolling Stoners' (Easy Rider), Neon **13** 9 108-113.
Hibbert, T. (1991) 'Dennis The Menace', Empire **30** 104-8.
Hill, L. (1996) Easy Rider (BFI Modern Classics, London).
Hodenfield, C. (1986) 'Citizen Hopper', Film Comment **22** (6) 62-73.
Hopper, D. (1986) Out of the Sixties (Twelvetrees Press, Pasadena).
Hunter, J. (1999) Dennis Hopper Movie Top Ten (Creation Books, London).
Kelley, B. (1988) 'True Colors', American Film **XII** (5) 19-22.
Martin, A. (1987) 'Dennis Hopper: Out of the Blue and Into the Black', Cinema Papers **74** 28-33.
Noever, P. (ed.) (2001) Dennis Hopper – A System Of Moments (Hatje Canz Verlag, Ostfildern-Ruit).
Nolan, T. (1970) 'You Can Bring Dennis Hopper to Hollywood But You Can't Take the Dodge City out of Kansas, Show **1** (9) 20-7.
Scharres, B. (1983) 'From Out of the Blue: The Return of Dennis Hopper', The Journal of the University Film and Video Association **35** (2) 25-31.
Stern, S. (2000) 'Writing Rebel

Where to start? Maybe with Sean Connery who put his head on the chopper by agreeing to be interviewed for the Scene by Scene pilot. On the strength of that, Mark Thompson commissioned the first series and became a most perceptive patron.

Carol Davidson was an unflappable first production manager and Des O'Hare, the first lighting cameraman, had a lasting influence on the images in this book. Anna Hursthouse was the researcher on the bulk of the interviews; her dedication and sense of detail still shows. She was a hard act to follow, but Becky Brazil more than managed it, bringing her great taste and energy to the task. She contributed directly to this book. Aileen Wild has calmly managed a gradually restricted budget from series two onwards with skill beyond my understanding. In the last few years, Buck Henry has been our series consultant. He benefited not one jot from this process, but we did, immeasurably. Over the same period, producer Pauline Law has handled a sometimes stroppy director and the BBC's swinging pendulum. The diplomatic corps is missing a trick, but television needs her. May Miller has executive produced from day one and Jane Root has continued to back us with money to film together with slots on her evolving BBC2. BBC4's Roly Keating has now taken over the baton.

Many other lighting camera-people, Pierre Olivier Bonasse, Stephen Broadhurst, Phil Dawson, Kris Denton, Danny Dimitroff, Simon Fanthorpe, Anne-Marie Fendrick, Ewan Gardner, John Halliday, Ed Kadysewsky, Ross Keith, Peter Loring, Mark Molesworth, Allan Palmer, Alan Smith, David Smith, Nick Squires and Tom Streithorst joined the Scene by Scene posse; the images, lighting and framing between these covers are often theirs. One of the least detectable influences on the book are the television version's editors, Jim Howat and in particular Donna Blackney. She set the grammar of our cutting and often judged the audience better than I. Jan Leman spent many hours reprinting grabs and helping me select the images in this volume.

The guests initially gave permission for their interview to be transmitted just once in the United Kingdom. Each has subsequently and without payment agreed to extracts being published here. Most were not on a publicity junket in the first place, so it was good of them to give up an afternoon. That they then lent personal photographs and have now waived rights to this book is beyond the call of duty.

Some years before the television version, I started Scene by Scene at the Edinburgh International Film Festival, in front of live audiences. Ginnie Atkinson, Angie Jennings, Susan Kemp and Fergus Robb backed the idea and polished it. Then and since, GLM has been great.

I mentioned the idea for this book to Alexander Ballinger and Gavin McLean in Edinburgh. They immediately went for it and have been indefatigable ever since. Alexander's knowledge and sense of detail is remarkable. The book is here because of them. My thanks also to NB:Studio and in particular to Ian Pierce for his meticulous contribution to the book's design. The proofreading was carried out efficiently by Patty Rennie and James Irvine. Carrie Forbes, my assistant editor, quietly brought all the transcripts together. She almost invisibly edited this book and the descriptions of many of the scenes are hers.

The following double page illustrations were kindly provided by the British Film Institute. Lauren Bacall in a 1940s publicity shot, pp.20-1; Jack Lemmon and Marilyn Monroe in Some Like it Hot (1959), pp.50-1; James Coburn, Robert Vaughn, Steve McQueen, Yul Brynner, Horst Buchholz, Charles Bronson and Brad Dexter on-set in The Magnificent Seven (1960), pp.58-9; Julie Christie, Donald Sutherland and Nicolas Roeg between takes in Don't Look Now (1973), pp.108-9; Brian De Palma behind the camera during the filming of Obsession (1976), pp.146-7 and Jonathan Demme directing Jodie Foster in The Silence of the Lambs (1991), pp.166-7.

Mark Cousins
Edinburgh, 2002.